Sticks & Stones Exposed

The Power of Our Words

dave weber

ISBN: 0-9760628-0-1

LCCN: 2004111053

This book includes information from many sources and personal experiences. It is intended to be used as a guide and a resource for its readers and is not intended to replace or substitute professional counseling or therapy where necessary. The publisher and author do not claim any responsibility or liability, directly or indirectly, for information or advice presented. While the publisher and author have made every effort to ensure the accuracy and completeness of the material, we claim no responsibility for potential inaccuracies, omissions, incompleteness, error, or inconsistencies.

Cover design and photos by Kevin Heffner.

Acknowledgements

When a book is more than three decades in the making, there are many people to thank. I first want to thank my father, Bob Weber, for both teaching and modeling for me the powerful principles in these pages. Dad, your ever-present challenge to "learn it, love it, and live it" has had such a profound impact on my life. You are one of the world's greatest Frog Kissers and I am so blessed to have had you as a father, teacher, role model, and best friend.

To my bride and biggest cheerleader, Tina, I want to thank you for your constant support and encouragement. You believed in me when I didn't believe in myself and you were an instrumental part in the birth of this book. Lindsey and Logan, thanks for the sacrifices you made while Dad was busy writing and the kitchen table was a mess of manuscripts.

To the great team at Weber Associates: Thom Suddreth, Chris Ivey Smith, Eddie Williams, Kevin Heffner, Jenny Hutchins, and Becky Pitts, thanks for all of your help. Without your constant affirmation and ideas, this project would have never happened.

And last, I especially want to thank a great writer and friend, Blane Bachelor. Your tireless efforts helped to transform my thoughts, ideas, and beliefs into the printed word. Blane, I enjoyed working on this with you and could never have tackled this book without your skill as a writer or insight as a person. Thank you for partnering with me to make Sticks and Stones a reality.

Dedication

This book is dedicated to Frog Kissers everywhere . . .
You make this world a better place.

Table of Contents

Chapter 1

Sticks and Stones

An injury is much sooner forgotten than an insult.
- Lord Chesterfield

The brisk New England wind whistled loudly through the trees that cold afternoon as seven-year-old Davey raced home from school, but the only thing he could hear was the chilling echo of his classmates' taunts. *"SHRIMPUS! SHRIMPUS!"* the other boys and girls shrieked over and over just moments ago, chanting in a frenzied mob at the bus stop. The word crushed Davey's heart like a sledgehammer on limestone. He ran from the bus stop as fast as he could, the wind whipping at his face, his tears nearly frozen as they streamed from his eyes, his spirit as dark and gray as the winter sky.

He finally arrived home, flinging open the door and heading toward the comfort and solitude of his bedroom. But his tear-streaked cheeks gave away his troubles as he tried to slip past his father, who gathered him up and asked what was wrong. Davey began sobbing again as he relived the horrible episode: the taunts, the teasing, the scathing nickname he knew he'd never forget. "Son," his father said, bending down to his level and pulling him close, "you need to remember that sticks and stones may break your bones, but names will never hurt you."

"But, Daddy," Davey sniffled, looking up at his father with teary blue eyes. "They *did* hurt me. They hurt me in my heart."

More than thirty winters have come and gone since I sought comfort in the arms and words of my father that day. While his hug soothed me, his words didn't. Even as a seven-year-old boy, I knew they weren't true – after all, that was real pain I felt, even though it didn't leave a visible bruise or scar.

Looking back now, I can laugh at the nickname "Shrimpus." It's actually kind of funny, and it was certainly appropriate – I was a small kid, and I'm still a relatively small guy. But although I chuckle about the episode now, I still remember every vivid detail of that cold day at the bus stop, when I learned my first real lesson about the power of words.

> *"Sticks and stones may break your bones,*
> *But names will never hurt you."*

Like my father, many of us reference this little phrase when we're trying to console someone we care about after they've been "hurt in their heart." "Sticks and stones" is a mantra handed down from generation to generation, helping children deal with the sting of the big, cruel world and the nasty people they'll inevitably encounter in it. Our hearts are in the right place in trying to help kids rationalize their hurt feelings with that little rhyme, but the logic isn't. Names *do* hurt – in fact, according to some research, emotional pain is processed in the same part of the brain as physical pain.

Broken bones mend themselves but harmful words and behaviors can result in lifelong injury.

And that emotional pain can result in something much worse than a broken bone. Broken bones mend themselves, sometimes growing stronger than they were before, but harmful words and behaviors can result in lifelong injury. They break our hearts, scratch our spirits, and dent our self-esteem, all of which is damage that may never fully heal. That damage can also manifest itself in detrimental physical ways.

A study done in 1999 by W. Penn Handwerker, a professor of anthropology at the University of Connecticut, Storrs, linked depression, suicide, stress, heart disease, and even the aggression witnessed in the Littleton, Colorado, public school shootings with a lifetime of harboring hurtful words from others. Handwerker's research looked at the effects of childhood violence – not just physical violence like hitting or slapping – but belittling and demeaning behavior, treating someone as inferior, and attempting to make people feel bad about themselves. Handwerker's research is just one of dozens of studies that have illustrated the incredible impact of negative words.

Clearly, words matter. They're powerful. And what matters most is *how* we use them. Do we use them like sticks and stones, to tear down, to destruct, and destroy? Or, do we use them to build up, encourage, and affirm?

A Rising Epidemic

The power of words is not a new or revolutionary concept. English novelist Edward George Bulwer Lytton, who died in 1873, once wrote, "The pen is mightier than the sword." Go thousands of years further back and you find the wisdom of King Solomon, "Death and life are in the power of the tongue . . ." In a more modern-day light, we were taught as youngsters the premise of the

What's so amazing about words is that they're so easily uttered, yet so difficult to forget.

Golden Rule, perhaps the most mainstream and timeless ethical standard for behavior. It states "Do unto others as you would have them do unto you" (I can't think of any healthy, self-respecting individual who would consider name-calling or belittling, negative statements – all of which are forms of sticks and stones – as part of behavior he or she would like directed at them). There are also countless examples in pop culture that address the potential impact of words. In Cher's 1980s hit, "If I Could Turn Back Time," she sings, "Words are like weapons; they wound sometimes."

What's so amazing about words is that they're so easily uttered, yet so difficult to forget once they've been tossed out there. While most of us can't even recall the details of our day-to-day life experiences – what we ate for dinner last Thursday, which clothes we wore on Monday, what we did last weekend – our minds act like virtual VCRs when it comes to the spoken word. They harbor a collection of all those ugly things people have said to us, effortlessly recording and playing back mean comments from years and years ago, even if the person who did the damage may not remember it a few days later. And, on the flip side, the positive, uplifting, supportive words stick in our minds, too. I'll bet every person reading this book has their own recollection of something especially positive a teacher, parent, or friend once said to them. We reflect on those comments, praise, and encouragements throughout our lives, whether we were five or fifty when we heard them.

> Our minds act like virtual VCRs when it comes to the spoken word.

Unfortunately, though, it seems the negative stuff is much more prevalent these days. Sticks and stones are being tossed all over the place. Just take a peek into any high school setting, where a snappy "dis" is considered much cooler than an honest compliment any day. An estimated 117 million Americans listen to or share gossip about other people at least once or twice a week, according to a poll commissioned by the non-profit organization WordsCanHeal.org. Flip on a television and take your pick of evidence: talk shows whose guests are verbally bashing each other in front of a national audience, reality shows with contestants who criticize teammates and cut down opponents on a regular basis. Road rage, a nonexistent term less than ten years ago, has become an everyday word in our vocabularies, as stressed-out drivers hurl streams of threats, insults, and obscenities at one another during rush hour traffic.

The examples go on and on. Researchers estimate that hundreds of thousands of children are teased and taunted every day at school. Rudeness is on the rise nationwide, according to a two-year survey released in 2002 called "Aggravating Circumstances: A Status Report on Rudeness in America." Conducted by Public Agenda, a nonprofit research arm of The Pew Charitable Trusts, this extensive survey found a whopping 79 percent of Americans say a lack of respect and courtesy should be regarded as a serious national problem – and 60 percent say that things are getting worse. Recently, some behavioral experts have coined a term, relational aggression, or RA, that suggests a disturbing trend developing among youngsters. It describes a variety of behaviors engaged in by children that harm others by damaging, or threatening to damage, one's relationship with his or her peers. Found to be more common in girls than boys, RA can be spreading rumors, purposefully ignoring others, or telling others not to play with a certain individual.

There's so much nastiness out there that some entrepreneur has made a fast buck off a simple but true societal slogan splashed on T-shirts and bumper stickers everywhere: "Mean People Suck." And then there's the related nationwide epidemic of increasing violence, in our schools, on our streets, and sometimes even in our homes.

Not a pretty picture, is it? So why can't we just drop our sticks, let our stones fall to the ground, and *all just get along?*

The answer is – as you're about to discover – because just getting along involves a lot more than we realize.

Even Golden Rule Gurus Need Help

You might be thinking, *Well, I'm not one of those mean people they talk about on bumper stickers. I don't ever exhibit road rage. I'm not part of that national rudeness epidemic. I live my life by the Golden Rule and I always treat other people with respect and encouragement!*

Good for you! I hope you're right. But consider this:

- ○ Have you ever found yourself the *target* of sticks and stones thrown out by others **who had no clue** about the damaging consequences of their words or actions?
- ○ Have you told a friend, a boss, a spouse: "I felt very hurt by what you said/did/conveyed through your behavior?"
- ○ Have you ever thought, "I didn't like how that person treated me?" or "His words really stung?"

If that's the case, isn't there at least a chance that you've done the same exact thing to someone else, without even realizing it either?

Even if you're not the kind of person who fires off snappy wisecracks, insulting remarks, or degrading comments like rocks from a slingshot, I'm willing to bet that at some point in your life your words or behaviors have hurt those around you. After all, actions can mean omissions too: They can be the things you don't do, you forget to do, or you simply don't think are important. When was the last time you told your child that she has brought so much joy into your life? Or your husband that you appreciate all his hard work? Or your co-worker that she did a great job on her presentation?

Your non-verbal behavior is just as important. What kind of message might you be sending with your basic body language? Without saying a word, we can throw sticks and stones at those around us. With rolled eyes. With crossed arms. With sighs. Even with silence.

If any of the above sounds familiar, you'll definitely get something out of this book. And even if you've already told yourself that the above paragraphs don't exactly describe you – you're a boss who praises her employees regularly; a husband who tells his wife she looks beautiful every day; a parent who encourages his children constantly – my hope is that this book will help you, too, by allowing you to discover a more effective way of affirming others in your life.

Therein lies one of my primary objectives in writing this book: to be a catalyst for some positive changes in your life. Changed perspectives. Changed beliefs. Ultimately, changed relationships and lives.

Intentional Affirmation

A few years ago, talk show icon and national celebrity Oprah Winfrey aired an episode that remains one of her most memorable to date. It featured "random acts of kindness" – unprompted, benevolent gestures that included paying the toll of the following car at the toll booth or anonymously donating sums of money to charity. This particular show made quite an impact on both the people who were featured as well as Oprah's viewing audience, causing a domino-like effect of positive behavior. People who'd been granted the "random acts" often returned the favor immediately, paying the fare for the car behind them, donating money to a charitable cause, or performing similar simple, kind acts for others.

When we hear about the kind actions of our fellow humans like this, it often strikes some sort of a good-nature chord within our spirits, doesn't it? We're awash in the warm glow of the decency of human nature, and we often feel moved enough to do some good of our own.

Furthermore, don't we say that an underlying motivation for various forms of altruism – treating others with kindness, volunteering our time, even offering a simple smile to a stranger on the street – is the sense of happiness *we* feel in doing such things? In other words, it's not just that we're making someone else's world brighter; it's the sense of accomplishment, of satisfaction, that indescribable "feel-good" factor that really inspires our own philanthropic efforts.

My point in all of this: If affirming others is so positive for us and our lives – not to mention the lives of those whom we are affirming – we need to do it intentionally, with purpose, all the time. What I'm talking about is a *conscious decision* to support, encourage, and lift up others every day of our lives. These concepts go beyond just dishing out an offhanded compliment here or a random act of kindness there. It's deeper than that.

But it's not rocket science, either. And I'm not spouting off some far-fetched, left-field hypotheses about human nature. My ideas are fairly simple, supported by a combination of research, common-sense knowledge, trends in society, and even some ancient literature. Once I started exploring these concepts a little bit further, I found evidence of their power everywhere I looked. In interactions among colleagues at my office. At the dinner table. At PTA meetings at my children's schools. Even between strangers in the doctor's office.

One . . . Two . . . Three . . .

Before we go any further, we need to go over three points you need to keep in mind while reading. These will help you understand and apply the concepts I'll be discussing.

1). You are a whole person. You may often define yourself in terms of your occupation, background, marital status, or hobbies, but those are just separate aspects of your life. However, you're not *just* an employee, *just* a parent, or *just* a friend – who you are as a person relates to the unique combination of all those different roles. The principles we'll discuss apply across the board to these roles in your life. You can apply them at the conference table, at the dinner table, and everywhere in between. And I encourage you to use them as widely as you can – they're much too powerful and effective to confine to just one area.

2). You have a *desire* to learn. Let's face it: I'm not naive enough to think that every one of you reading this book picked it up on your own – you might be reading it as suggested by your manager or spouse (in which case, please keep reading – you'll end up thanking them for it, I promise!). Whatever the case – if you're here for fun, by force, or for personal interest – you're here because your goal is to learn something.

3). You're a changing person. In the words of 1920s advertising baron Bruce Barton, "When you're through changing, you're through." If you haven't heard that phrase before, you've certainly heard this one (or some version of it): "The only constant in life is change." If change is a given, then what I hope to influence is the direction of that change. Which way are you headed in your emotional and behavioral development as a person? Are you progressing or regressing? By sharing these principles, I hope to push you on a forward-moving track.

One last note before we dig in: All of the stories and anecdotes in this book are based on actual experiences and events. However, some names have been omitted or changed.

Chapter 2

The Bamboo Tube Challenge

Men are anxious to improve their circumstances, but are unwilling
to improve themselves; therefore, they remain bound.
        - James Allen

*W*hat does this blob look like to you? A Rorschach inkblot?
A minor oil spill? A major printing error?

It could be all of those things, but if you step back, way
back, from that black spot, you might see something entirely
different.

Like a leopard, perhaps? Turn back to the previous page, where you were able to see just one part of that leopard – one of its spots. But now, when you step back and look at it from a wider perspective, you can see it as the whole creature it really is.

This visual stems from the words of Charlie Chan, the old Chinese detective, who said, "Man only sees one spot on a leopard when he looks through a bamboo tube." I collect sayings and quotations, and Chan's is one of my favorites. While I admit it doesn't exactly ring of brilliance, its beauty lies in the meaning it takes on when you look at it in broader terms. Maybe you've heard the idea expressed another way: "He's got the blinders on," "She has tunnel vision," or "You can't see the forest for the trees."

These expressions all relate to the same concept – that taking a step back from something reveals a whole different point of view. Let's examine Chan's original quote a little further. Are you looking at the leopard – a metaphor for your life, really – through a bamboo tube? If that's the case, when that leopard takes a huge chomp out of your backside and you feel excruciating pain, it's doubtful you'll have any clue about the real source of the pain. That's because all you can see is that one black spot – instead of the entire animal with its teeth sunk into your flesh.

Sometimes, we go through our personal life journeys in much the same way. So many of us aspire to do great things with our lives – to achieve, to serve, to create, to love, to inspire. But don't many of us, at one point or another, find ourselves being devoured by our responsibilities, our circumstances, our situations, our environments, and our careers, to the point where we wake up one day and find that the joy we once felt about those things isn't there?

I think this happens because we're often so focused on just one aspect of our lives that when we feel hurt or numb or unfulfilled – chomped on the backside by that leopard – we have no idea why, because we're not looking at everything from a big-picture standpoint. It's like a doctor who prescribes painkillers for a patient's recurring headaches without exploring other possibilities for the cause of the pain. If the doctor had diagnosed the patient with a holistic approach, maybe he would have found that the underlying source of her headaches is depression and stress, which require deeper treatment than just popping a pill.

So let's put that bamboo tube down. Let's take the blinders off our eyes. Let's look around a bit and shake off the tunnel vision so we *can* see the forest, despite all the trees.

When we do so, we can see others and ourselves in a whole different light. That new sense of vision allows us to reconnect with others where we've been disconnected for so long – in our jobs, in our marriages, in our relationships with our children, friends, teammates, neighbors.

The principles in this book are based on using that kind of vision. Once you start using it, you'll begin to see your life, and every relationship and interaction you have, in an entirely new light.

Chapter 3

The Koinonia Connection

We were born to unite with our fellow men, and to join in community with the human race.
- Cicero

$\mathcal{H}$abitat for Humanity is a world-renowned organization that provides shelter for underprivileged people and their families. Based in Americus, Georgia, this incredible non-profit has warmed hearts across the globe through its mission to build homes for people who would never be able to afford houses otherwise. A similar group is Rebuilding Together, which was founded under the original name of Christmas in April. The objective of this national organization is similar to that of Habitat, but instead of starting from scratch to build a house, Rebuilding Together rehabilitates already existing homes for low-income families and individuals.

It was at one of those rebuilding events several years ago that I first heard the word *koinonia* (coy-non-EE-ah), and I liked it so much I've been using it in my material ever since. Koinonia is a Greek term that translates most closely as "community." But koinonia relates more to a concept that doesn't have literal definition in English. It's kind of like the Hawaiian word "aloha," which is used as both hello and goodbye, but also encompasses the helpful spirit of the Hawaiian community. There's also "irie" in Jamaica, which roughly means things are cool, everything's all right. In Costa Rica, the catch phrase "pura vida" literally means "pure life," but "pura vida" really sums up the Central American country's laid-back, naturalistic lifestyle and is used in infinite ways in local Spanish.

Similar to those expressions, koinonia really can't be translated into a single word. Rather, it covers four concepts: community, communication, communion, and fellowship. But even these words don't quite get to the core of koinonia. Over the years, I have expanded these concepts to create my own personal definition of koinonia: "the coming together in a solidified one-ness in an atmosphere of openness, honesty, trust, affirmation, support, and encouragement."

Koinonia: 'the coming together in a solidified one-ness in an atmosphere of openness, honesty, trust, affirmation, support, and encourgement.'

Wow. Re-read that definition again and really let it sink in. Isn't that the kind of environment we'd love to have in any relationship? An environment in which all of our interactions are open and honest and trusting and affirming and supportive and encouraging?

I've yet to find a term in the English language that fully encapsulates all those things koinonia stands for. We tend to use more shallow descriptions of our relationships. If we're lucky enough to be well-connected with others in our lives, we say we have "strong" marriages with our spouses. Or "good working relationships" with our colleagues. Or, we're "tight" with our buddies. But what do those definitions really mean?

If you take an analytical approach, you would probably describe those relationships with some of the same words that help to define koinonia: trust, honesty, encouragement, and support. Koinonia allows us to grow as people, to have the courage and support necessary to reach our dreams and achieve our potential, to feel connected with and be a part of the world around us – all of the wonderful stuff that makes us happy humans. Koinonia connections with others are an essential ingredient in full, enriched lives.

But, sad to say, those vital koinonia connections are many times absent in our lives. While koinonia *can* exist in any of these relationships, all too often it doesn't.

- Between a wife and a husband
- Between a boss and an employee
- Between a parent and a child
- Between a coach and a player
- Between a teacher and a student
- Between friends

No Cookie-Cutter Koinonia

It's important to note that koinonia, when it *does* develop, can look very different depending on the relationship. Being open with your spouse ("I know you have some issues with my family, honey, but it would really make me happy if you could just *pretend* to like them") is a lot different than being open with your employees ("We need to work on your customer relation skills"). You encourage your best friend with one approach ("Go ahead – ask her out! You look awesome tonight!") and your co-workers with another ("You should definitely apply for that upcoming position in management"). You support your teammates ("Way to crush that ball, Mike! You're the MAN!") in different ways than you support your children ("You're doing such a wonderful job with your chores around the house, sweetheart"). In other words, koinonia is not an all-encompassing, sweeping concept that applies to all of our relationships in the same way.

Nor does koinonia mean we have to be best buddies with everyone who crosses our path. Sometimes, you may not even like the people that you're interacting with in certain situations – but keep in mind that you can still achieve koinonia with them. Of course, liking each other helps. But if that's not necessarily the case (I sense some of you out there in Corporate America nodding), remember that koinonia is contingent upon principles other than just basic levels of compatibility. Instead, it's about establishing openness, honesty, trust, affirmation, support, and encouragement. With that foundation in place, koinonia can develop anywhere – even with people you perhaps consider rivals or enemies. (Though I'd be willing to bet that once you start building true koinonia connections with those people, it won't be long before your opinions of them start changing!)

It's Not All or Nothing

Unless you're Greek or a language expert, this is probably the first time you've ever heard of koinonia. And while you might not have recognized them, you've probably seen koinonia connections at their finest. They form the basis of companies whose executives treat their employees like human beings instead of drones – and have impressive bottom-line profits to show for it. They're the lifeblood of marriages that seem so magical they almost glow with love and respect. They exist in parent-child bonds strong enough to survive even the teenage years with everyone's limbs intact.

Achieving koinonia is a process; like a fine wine, it needs time to develop. Naturally, with any relationship – whether it's romantic, platonic, professional, or just a casual acquaintance – the levels of support, honesty, and trust that form the basis of koinonia are relatively nonexistent to begin with. In other words, koinonia doesn't burst onto the scene the moment we meet someone. But as two people get to know each other better, their connection begins to deepen. Over time, the path toward koinonia becomes clearer if those two individuals interact with one another based on shared levels of trust, honesty, support, and all the other good stuff koinonia is made of.

It can happen conversely, too. As two people get know each other, they might find that they don't necessarily like each other. For whatever reason – it could be a personality conflict, a difference of opinions or values, or just a little competitive friction here and there – some hostility begins to develop between these people. Consequently, their constant negative interactions begin to move them farther and farther away from the koinonia ideal. They're not supportive of one another. They don't treat each other with respect or encouragement. And they certainly aren't trusting of each other. All of which makes a prime environment for lots of sticks and stones, and less koinonia.

It's also important to note that with respect to koinonia, every relationship is dynamic. Like a wooden bead that slides back and forth across an abacus, all relationships are either moving closer toward or farther away from koinonia. This is what I call the koinonia continuum. It means that every action and reaction we make in relation to others in our lives – an unreturned phone call to a friend, a birthday bouquet of flowers for the receptionist, a disapproving glance at an employee as he creeps in late – either help develop koinonia with that person, or detract from it. No action, however minute or grandiose, comes without some effect on the koinonia continuum.

> No action, however minute or grandiose, comes without some effect on the koinonia continuum.

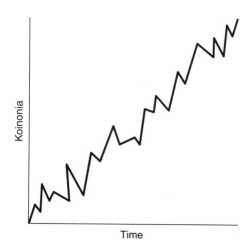

Time

Think about where you'd place your relationships on the koinonia continuum. Are some close to the koinonia ideal? Are others, by comparison, way far off the radar? What about your actions and behaviors – are they bringing you closer toward koinonia with others, or pushing you farther apart?

Keep in mind that koinonia involves more than the destination – it's the trip to get there. It's more than a product – it's a process. We need to understand and appreciate the process and the trip, not just the destination. In other words, just because you haven't attained or achieved koinonia with another person, that doesn't mean the relationship is a failure. What's infinitely more important is the direction in which you're moving.

> Keep in mind that koinonia involves more than the destination – it's the trip to get there. It's more than a product – it's a process.

Maslow and Koinonia

According to the late psychologist Abraham Maslow, connections with others are a basic need of human beings. Remember Maslow and his famous hierarchy of needs? In the first widespread publication of the needs hierarchy in 1954, Maslow mapped out his famous layered pyramid structure, which established an order of needs that humans are biologically and physiologically programmed to achieve before moving up to the next level. Other studies had theorized about a similar setup of human needs, but Maslow's scheme was revolutionary in its maintenance of needs in an orderly, ascending fashion. In other words, until one level of needs is met, achieving or attaining those needs is the only motivating factor for behavior at that point. Only after a person has met his needs at the first level can he advance to the second, and so on.

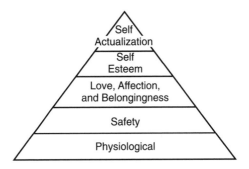

First on the list at the base of the pyramid, Maslow maintained, is the need to obtain the most basic of human needs – food, water, sleep, sex. Next, comes the need for safety, whose components include protection from violence, shelter, law and order, and social stability. (Some psychologists have asserted that the security needs should be grouped with Maslow's basic physiological needs.)

At the *very next level* is the need for love and belonging. The need to feel accepted. The need to feel a part of relationships with others – which is essentially the need for koinonia connections.

Our need to feel accepted by and connected with others shows up in everyday examples all the time. It helps explain why people seek out and join groups like fraternities, sororities, alumni associations, bingo clubs, and even street gangs. Of course, there's usually a common thread of interest that forms the basis of the group. But what we're really looking for goes beyond a desire to hone our bingo skills or get together with other baseball fans to watch the game – we're trying to find that special sense of belonging. We yearn for acceptance. We want to fit in and be liked by others. In other words, we ultimately crave those koinonia connections.

As Maslow's theories suggested, feeling connected to others is such a basic human need that in the absence of another human to connect with, we'll turn to whatever we can. Remember Tom Hanks' character, Chuck Noland, in the hit movie "Castaway"? Stranded on a remote desert island after a horrendous airplane wreck, Chuck helped keep his sanity intact by interacting with a volleyball – which he named Wilson – that had washed up on the shore.

Of course, even though he was likely suffering some mental meltdowns as a result of his seemingly hopeless situation, Chuck hadn't regressed into thinking that he'd gain acceptance from or be liked by an inanimate object. What Chuck was going for was a basic semblance of human interaction, even though he was the only one doing the talking. Beyond giving the volleyball a name, he gave it a human-esque face created out of a bloody handprint. He placed Wilson where he could see it every day, talking to it and asking it questions, and even experienced an emotional breakdown triggered when Wilson floated away during his escape.

But if, as research by Maslow and countless other human behavioral experts suggests, we're hard-wired to need these strong ties with other people, especially in extreme situations like Chuck's, why aren't we experiencing more koinonia connections in our lives? Why do so many spouses have such a difficult time communicating with one another, making people like John Gray, author of bestseller *Men are From Mars, Women are From Venus*, very rich folks? Why does the generation gap between parents and children sometimes feel more like the Continental Divide? Why would so many employees prefer to pull out their own molar teeth with a pair of rusty pliers than have lunch with their supervisors?

Koinonia Disconnections

Now that we understand how everyone is hard-wired to desire and need koinonia connections with other people, here's what drives us crazy: It's all these people that keep getting in the way! It sounds contradictory, but yes, it's all these others that make establishing true koinonia so difficult.

It's similar to the school teacher who says, "I would love my job so much more if I just didn't have to deal with these students!" Or the sales rep who says, "This gig would be so great if I didn't have customers!" But being an educator is dependent on having students to teach, and being a sales rep means having customers – defining those professions is contingent on the people they interact with. In the same way, we need others in order to have koinonia connections; they don't exist in a vacuum.

However, when it comes to interacting effectively with others, it's often like we're trying to square-dance with ski boots on. It's awkward. It's difficult. And we keep tripping over ourselves – and each other. But there's a reason it's so tricky: We're not communicating with just one person – we really have *seven* others to contend with! *What?!*, you say?

> When it comes to interacting effectively with others, it's often like we're trying to square dance with ski boots on.

I believe there are actually seven versions of ourselves living inside of each and every one of us. Let me first clarify: I am not talking about multiple personalities or a demonic possession issue (I'll leave those topics to trained psychologists and Stephen King). It might sound a little off the wall at first, but I think we all have seven concepts of self that together help to define who we are as a person. Just like we often look at ourselves as a sum of our different roles – manager, swimmer, father, basketball fan – our composite as a human being results from the integration of seven concepts of self that reside within each of us. I call them the **Seven Me's.**

Once you begin to understand how these Seven Me's work within you, you can better understand how they work within other people. This insight ultimately opens the door for significantly greater fulfillment in all of our relationships as we begin to realize the complex communication dynamic involved in every interaction. You see, here's the challenge: When two people get together, there are not just two people talking. There are actually fourteen Me's running around – seven in one person, and seven in the other. Add a third person to the conversation and you can have *twenty-one* Me's trying to influence the interaction! No wonder relationships can get so complicated.

This train of thought is not new. Concepts of self have long been a subject of interest for psychologists and sociologists, generating volumes of research, studies, and journals on the topic. Sigmund Freud, the German behavioral scientist known as the father of psychology, theorized three separate concepts of self – the Id, the Ego, and the Superego – that predicate behavior and form the basis of our personalities. Author Thomas Harris also described three in his best-selling book, *I'm OK, You're OK: A Practical Guide to Transactional Analysis*: the parent, child, and adult aspects of our nature as human beings.

Freud, Harris, and countless other experts on personality and human nature devoted their professional lives to researching topics related to the various aspects of self, but my approach is a little bit different. I'm not going to dig into convoluted theories, data, or psycho-babble. Instead, I've outlined the principles more in layman's terms, resulting from years of observation of relationships in all aspects of life: the corporate world, the family arena, and everyday social interaction.

Rather than exploring these concepts from only a "self-reflection, what-do-you-see-in-the-mirror" perspective, we will discover how the perceptions of others can positively or negatively influence who we are, and therefore, how we behave. Consequently, it's crucial to understand the role others play in the formation of our concepts of self and, whether we realize it or not, to recognize that we play a similar role in shaping theirs.

The Many Me's I Am

When I began studying and speaking about this subject to organizations across the country, I thought I had uncovered a topic not many people knew about. I did research, spoke with personality experts, and did lots of reading, but nowhere could I find information that identified the concepts of self, or the Seven Me's, as I visualized them. Then I ran across the following poem that was written quite some time ago.

Four Men
It chanced upon a winter's night,
Safe sheltered from the weather,
The board was spread for only one,
Yet four men dined together.
There sat the man I meant to be,
In glory, spurred and booted,
And close beside him, to the right,
The man I am reputed.
The man I think myself to be
His seat was occupying
Hard by the man I really am,
Who to hold his own was trying.
And all beneath one roof we met,
Yet none called his fellow brother.
No sign of recognition passed –
They knew not one another.
– Unknown

I had been scooped – by a poem with language suggesting it was hundreds of years old, no less! This wise, unknown author was describing a phenomenon that still very much applies to our modern-day lives. Though he or she only addressed four of the seven concepts of self I'll be talking about, the real essence of his poem lies in the fact that none of these "Four Men" had an inkling of awareness about each other. We tend to operate in the same way. Though we may reflect on the kind of people we once were or the ideal person we'd like to become – all of which are components of the many Me's we are – many of us, like the four men in the poem, have yet to sit down to dinner with all seven at once. So, without further ado, I'd like to introduce you to your Seven Me's.

The Seven Me's

The Me I Think I Am
The Me I Really Am
The Me I Used to Be
The Me Others See
The Me I Try to Project
The Me Others Try to Make Me
The Me I Want to Be

Chapter 4

The Me I Think I Am

Know yourself. Don't accept your dog's admiration
as conclusive evidence that you are wonderful.
– Ann Landers

I have a **Me I Think I Am.** Don't you? Your kids definitely
have little Me's they think they are. You can see it in the way
they walk. Talk. Dress. Play with each other in the sandbox.
Your boss has a Me he thinks he is. You can see it in the way
he walks. Talks. Dresses. Winks at himself in the mirror.

But forget others for a second, and think back to a situation when you were asked to describe yourself in three
adjectives. Perhaps during a job interview. Maybe having a
cocktail with a friend. Or perhaps as a messy-haired grade
school kid, where you scribbled down your answers with a
crayon onto construction paper.

If you had to do it again right now, what words would
you use? Would you describe yourself in terms of your
appearance, your abilities, your outlook on life, or a combination of those and others? You would likely assess yourself
in terms of your roles in life: as an employee, as a parent, as a
sibling, as a boss, as a daughter, as a friend. Some of your
word choices would also likely reflect your relationships with
others: "loyal" or "independent." Perhaps, if you're really
honest about some of your weaknesses, you might include
words like "lazy" or "judgmental."

This simple exercise helps to define the Me I Think I Am. This Me is really a snapshot of how you see yourself right now, whether it's in a positive or negative light, or some combination of both. Still, this Me can be a tricky one to define. The word "think" implies that there's a margin for error, that the "real" me can vary from the one we imagine or think ourselves to be.

This Me is really a snapshot of how you see yourself right now.

Another way to look at this Me is by taking out some old photos of yourself – your high school senior class portrait is a good one. Think back to that time and try to remember how you felt as the person looking back at you (this took a while for me, because I couldn't stop laughing at my ridiculous ruffled tuxedo and big hair long enough to really think about much else). Did you view yourself as a confident, self-assured senior, ruling the school and ready to take on whatever "real world" challenges were awaiting you? Or were you a shy, timid teenager?

An Accurate View?

Many times, we believe the Me I Think I Am reflects an accurate picture of who we really are at the current point in time. But, looking back at ourselves – like when we pull out the high school portraits – we often discover that those assessments way back then didn't quite hit the mark. Perhaps we were the hotshot seniors, big and bad and ready to take on the world, only to find ourselves drowning at college shortly thereafter as a little fish in the proverbial big pond. Or maybe we were one of those "late bloomers," extremely shy and unconfident in our high school days, only to blossom into success stories with futures so bright we *should* have been wearing shades. In other words, in the present, we believe the Me I Think I Am is an accurate assessment of ourselves. But in hindsight, we often uncover how incomplete or inaccurate our self-perceptions were.

According to research, most of us harbor a distorted view of ourselves. And like those warped mirrors in carnival funhouses, the distortion is negative. Though the person we see in the mirror is horribly short or agonizingly tall, those reflections aren't an accurate picture of the real person standing in front of the mirror. In our lives, we tend to look at ourselves the same way. We see ourselves as less capable, less attractive, dumber, or less desirable than we really are.

Why are we so good at twisting the truth? Well, the answer is related to the way in which our brains process information. According to some research, our subconscious minds tend to focus on negative input and cues – which can be our own nasty, self-deprecating comments or the verbal sticks and stones others toss at us – instead of positive input and cues. But there's a reason for this kind of subconscious pessimism. Some researchers say it's likely related to a key function of the brain, which is to be on the lookout for potential threats in order to keep us alive and well. A potentially harmful side effect, though, is that this also plays a role in how we each develop our sense of self. If our brains tend to hang on to the negative stuff from our own thoughts and from others, our self-esteem – which is reflected by the Me I Think I Am – can begin to suffer.

The concept of the Me I Think I Am hinges somewhat on feedback from others, too. If you've spent any time in Corporate America, you've likely experienced one of those maddening self-evaluation appointments with your supervisor.

You know the drill: You have to rate yourself, usually on a points system, based on your communication skills, your ability to meet a deadline, how well you achieve goals, how often you re-fill the coffee pot in the break room. They're a nightmare, I know, but they also offer a practical illustration of the Me I Think I Am. Just as you'll often rate yourself differently on that evaluation than your boss or supervisor will, you have a different picture and description of yourself than others do.

Of course, this begins to touch on another Me you'll learn more about later – the Me Others See. But for now, it's important to recognize that when you consider the opinions and insight of others, differences will usually arise in the Me I Think I Am.

The American Idol, or the American Idiot?

At the time this book went to press, "American Idol" had finished its third season as one of the nation's most popular television shows. Most of you are familiar with how it works: A group of up-and-coming singing hopefuls, mostly teenagers and twenty-somethings, compete against each other week after week gunning for the final prize, which is a contract with a major record label and almost guaranteed instant fame.

As is the case (or curse) with many reality shows, "American Idol" can be maddeningly addictive. But perhaps the most fun part of the whole extravaganza is the early part of the season. This is when the show features not-yet-weeded-out contestants who have about as much right to be on the stage with a mike in their hand as I do to be atop a unicycle in a three-ring circus, balancing on a high tightrope while juggling flaming batons. I mean, let's be serious here! These poor souls, bless their hearts, sound like hyenas with bronchitis and emanate about as much stage presence as an actuary, but they honestly believe they have what it takes to become the next "American Idol."

At the same time, some of the most memorable shows are entire episodes based on the brutal criticism they take from the judges! While we cringe as they're pummeled with verbal sticks and stones from the judging panel, usually from the infamously honest Simon Cowell, we also can't help but scratch our heads and wonder how they could be so jaded about their talents.

> These poor souls sound like hyenas with bronchitis and emanate about as much stage presence as an actuary.

With respect to a truthful assessment of their natural abilities and potential futures in show business, these unfortunate contestants don't have much of a clue about the Me I Think I Am. In their minds, they're the next hot act to hit the music industry, but in reality, those judges – as well as anyone with their sense of hearing intact – know otherwise.

Everyday Examples

You don't have to turn on the television to find more examples of the inaccuracies that can arise with the Me I Think I Am. They're everywhere. It's a boss who thinks she's the most encouraging, supportive supervisor in the business world (her employees, especially those who have been passed over for promotions year after year, think otherwise). It's a parent who thinks he's the most laid-back, understanding dad in the country (his kids certainly have a different opinion). It's a husband who thinks he's the most affectionate, supportive spouse out there (while his wife's eyebrows raise so high they nearly float off her forehead).

One of my wife's favorite examples of the discrepancies in the Me I Think I Am involves our daughter's cheerleading coach. She is a great coach, don't get me wrong, but at one point, as far as the discipline, rules, and workouts went, she could have posed as a drill sergeant. Her students had to be exactly on time, to the minute, for every practice and event. They were expected to be in peak form for every stunt and routine.

Goals were set for every practice, and each workout was carefully scripted and timed to the minute. All of these characteristics were what helped her to be such a great coach. She planned her work and worked her plan – a plan from which she never wanted to deviate. She even went as far as to demand the exact shade of the hair ribbons the girls wore.

One time, this coach and my wife, Tina, were sitting next to each other at an out-of-town cheerleading competition, and they began chatting. At some point in the conversation, the coach mentioned that she was able to "go with the flow" about a friend's upcoming plans, because she was "flexible" about those sorts of things.

"You mean, you're flexible in terms of your relationships, right?" Tina asked.

"What do you mean?" the coach responded.

"Well . . ." Tina began explaining, as gently and tactfully as she could, that her perfectionist nature was sometimes a challenge to deal with. Turns out, the coach had no idea how inflexible she could be at times. The rest of the trip, she approached other parents and inquired, "Do you think I'm flexible?" In asking the question, she was trying to validate and substantiate her view of herself. In other words, she wanted to hear that she really was flexible because that was her Me I Think I Am. It was a tricky question for the parents to answer, but their reactions and responses also generated some pivotal feedback for the coach.

Eventually, the coach loosened up a little. She was still strict, mind you, but I believe the honest insight she received from Tina and other parents about the inaccuracy of her Me I Think I Am was a valuable tool in broadening her self-perception in her role as a coach. In the end, I think everyone – the coach, her students, the parents, and the team as a whole – benefited from it. In fact, she's come so far that "being flexible" is now a sort of running joke between her and some of the parents.

Digging Deeper

The Me I Think I Am is one of the most difficult of the Seven Me's to pinpoint – because no matter how we see ourselves, it's virtually impossible to get a completely precise picture without considering the input of others. Still, being aware of this Me allows us an opportunity for some self-discovery. It can offer some pivotal insight into the accuracy of our self-perceptions.

You think you're a laid-back, carefree parent? What, your kids don't quite agree? Think you're a good listener? Your spouse might have a completely different opinion. You'd describe your management style as hands-off? Your employees might snicker at the mere suggestion.

Find out why.

Advice to Stick With

Spend a day keeping your eyes and ears finely tuned for clues that might signal a discrepancy in your Me I Think I Am.

O Ask questions.
O Solicit feedback.
O Listen.

Chapter 5

The Me I Really Am

Your vision will become clear only when you can look into your own heart. Who looks outside, dreams; who looks inside, awakes.
– Carl Jung

To "know thyself," as Greek philosopher Socrates so simply but so aptly put it thousands of years ago, is a basic concept in philosophy and psychology as well as a fundamental human urge. Having some idea of who or what we are – **the Me I Really Am** – gives us insight, knowledge and understanding of our place in the world around us and helps us to determine how we should conduct ourselves in it. And the better we know and understand ourselves, the better we can understand others – because we're more able to recognize differences between us and similarities we share.

Discovering the Me I Really Am has become a hot topic in today's society. For years, behavioral experts have connected a high level of self-knowledge as contingent to our well-being, sense of purpose, and overall happiness. But only in recent years has a mainstream trend for self-discovery really caught fire. Self-help sections in bookstores virtually overflow with material enlightening us about how to find our true selves. Television show host Oprah Winfrey, radio personality and author Dr. Laura Schlessinger, and Dr. Phil McGraw, also a television show host and author, have achieved near celebrity-status (and quite an enviable living) by helping thousands of people to dig deep into the Me I Really Am. They are the catalyst for their guests, readers, and listeners to get a better understanding of the Me I Really Am. They prompt their guests to ask themselves difficult questions about decisions in their lives and to take a hard look into their behaviors and actions.

The Me I Really Am – do you have any insight about who or what this person is, what characteristics, values, and beliefs he or she encompasses? Do you truly know yourself?

According to Dr. P. Phillip Sidwell, a licensed industrial psychologist and former director of the Center for Professional Management Education at Georgia State University in Atlanta, you probably don't. And you're not alone. Through years of research and counseling hundreds of individuals, groups, and organizations of all ages, demographics, and socio-economic backgrounds, Sidwell observes that the overwhelming majority of us don't have deep insight into what makes us tick as individuals – in effect, what defines our "authentic" self. This is a concept referred to by many behavioral experts to describe the fascinating, but often largely undiscovered, combination of our passions, aspirations, values, fears, and goals in life. In other words, it's the unique formula that helps define our true identity – the Me I Really Am.

On the bright side, Sidwell's observations also suggest that since some of us, although a minority, do have insight about ourselves, the potential is there for those of us who are a bit in the dark to become enlightened. So why don't we? If so many of us don't have a good understanding of the Me I Really Am but *could* get to know that Me – why are we still relatively ignorant about this concept of self? Fear. I think we're afraid of what we might discover.

When it comes to self-discovery – taking a hard look at our-selves, at the kind of person, parent, boss, friend, employee, sibling we are – we tend to choose the bliss of ignorance over the pain of insight. It's like that trip to the doctor's office we keep putting off. Our body is telling us something is wrong, but we find it's easier to deal with if we don't know just how bad the problem is, because it might be pretty serious, requiring several follow-up visits, heavy medication, compli-cated treatment, or surgery. Rather than deal with the problem itself, we ignore it, continuing to reschedule the appointment while rationalizing the situation. *I'm fine. There's nothing wrong with me. Everything's okay.* Sound familiar?

> When it comes to self-discovery we tend to choose the bliss of ignorance over the pain of insight.

Similarly, when we think about aspects of our selves that we don't really like – whether it's that volatile temper or that madden-ing indecisiveness or that prickly demeanor at work – it's usu-ally painful. Admitting and facing up to our faults is difficult, and so many times we go to great lengths to avoid confronting them. Up go those defenses. We keep a tight lid on the Me I Really Am, because we're afraid to see our shortcomings, weaknesses, and faults lurking in the dark, shadowy corners.

It's a lot easier to avoid that kind of painful, but instru-mental, self-reflection in this everything-at-breakneck-speed, no-downtime, I'm-too-busy-to-even-breathe society most of us live in today. We have a full-time job to worry about! The kids to pick up at soccer practice!! Dinner to make!!! Time at the gym to squeeze in!!!! That report to finish!!!!! (And this is all on a *calm* day.) Being insanely busy has become such an accepted status in our fast-paced society that we almost feel guilty when – if ever – we finally do slow down.

Technology has played a huge role in this manic, Mach-speed pace of life we seem to be addicted to, but I believe many of us are also using that same technology – Palm Pilots®, cell phones, Blackberries®, high-speed Internet – as a kind of escapism from ourselves. With our lives in constant overdrive, we stay so busy being logged on and tuned in that we can be tuned out of true reflection into our lives . . .

> With our lives in constant overdrive, we stay so busy being logged on and tuned in that we can be tuned out of true reflection.

> . . . into what really makes us happy;
> . . . into why we're unhappy or dissatisfied;
> . . . into what drives us;
> . . . into what angers us;
> . . . into where our true passions lie;
> . . . into our deepest fears.

All of these help us define the Me I Really Am.

The BGI – A Pretty BIG Deal

Sometimes, when we stop all of our rushing around for a moment to pause, take a breath, and then take a good, hard look at ourselves, we get in return what I call a Blinding Glimpse of Insight, or a BGI. Much in the same way that we shield our eyes from bright sunlight, we usually shield our eyes from a BGI because it's a little piece of understanding or recognition about ourselves that hurts to look at. When we're in sticks-and-stones mode, we often do or say things that have consequences we don't even consider at the moment. A BGI is just one way we can be confronted with the potential ways those sticks and stones can damage others around us. In other words, a BGI is often the result when we take the bamboo tube away and look at the Me I Really Am from a big-picture standpoint.

Think of a BGI as someone shining a high-powered spotlight onto those actions, words, or behaviors and their negative consequences – consequences that we're usually unaware of. When that BGI hits us, whether someone else points it out or we take a hard look back at our actions and their effect on others, it's almost a scripted routine. Nine times out of ten, we slap our foreheads, sigh deeply, and say, or think, "I can't believe I did/said that!" That moment of recognition is like being smacked alongside the head with a giant two-by-four. And it hurts.

> We usually shield our eyes from a BGI because it's a little piece of understanding or recognition about ourselves that hurts to look at.

But we can learn from the pain that often results from honest insight into ourselves. I'm convinced that no amount of personal growth comes without a little bit of pain. Painful knowledge about ourselves is often the first step in the growth process. Once our negative words and behaviors have been exposed by the bright light of a BGI, the next step is change as we focus on eliminating and eradicating those negative words and behaviors.

From Soccer to Saddles

When I was a young man, soccer was my ticket in life. I earned honors as an All-Conference defender at NCAA Division I

Mercer University and was chosen as a captain for three years. Playing was my passion. I loved practice. I lived for games. I continued playing in competitive leagues after college. Soccer was everything to me for nearly a decade of my life.

But by the time my wife and I had our first child, I had hung up my cleats. So, of course, next in line to carry on the proud tradition of soccer I'd started was our six-year-old, Lindsey. During her first season, she wasn't very into the sport, but my wife and I figured she was just getting the hang of it. By the second season, she still hadn't shown much interest, but I didn't care. This was Lindsey Weber – the next-of-kin to the legendary Dave Weber, soccer player extraordinaire! She had hundreds of goals to score! Tournaments to win!! Scholarships to earn!!! Soccer was *it* for me, so of course, soccer had to be *it* for my daughter, too – right?

Wrong. My futbol-fanatic mindset clouded out any shred of possibility that maybe soccer just wasn't Lindsey's thing – until, finally, about halfway through her second season, a blisteringly bright BGI hit me on a rainy game day. Despite the bad weather, the "beehive" strategy was in full force, with the usual swarm of little legs poking and kicking the ball in the mass hovering all around the muddy field.

My daughter, however, was nowhere to be found in the swarm. Instead, she stood by herself several feet from the scrum, gazing off into the distance in a Zen-like trance. Across the field in the hive, the ball popped loose and rolled toward her.

"KICK IT!" I screamed from the sidelines like some sort of crazed Pygmy. *"LINDSEY, KICK THE BALL! KIIIIIIIII-ICK IIIIIIIT!"*

Lindsey seemed to snap from her reverie just in time to look down at the very moment the ball rolled right over her foot. By that time, the swarm had caught up, buzzing past her in a flurry of legs and feet and jerseys in chase of the ball. I almost fell out of the bleachers in agony, as my wife and mother-in-law exploded into gales of laughter. At halftime, I called my daughter over for a quick pep talk.

"Lindsey, *what are you doing* out there? Why didn't you *just kick the ball* when it came to you?" I pleaded desperately.

My daughter looked at me, her blue eyes gazing into mine, her little blond ponytail drenched from the showers. "Daddy?" she asked with a breezy wave of her hand, "wouldn't this field be so much prettier if there were horses out here?"

BAM. That BGI hit me, and everything was painfully clear. The BGI brought to light an agonizing aspect of my Me I Really Am – I even remember thinking to myself something along the lines of, "You selfish, ignorant, buffoon of a father." Instead of letting my daughter discover her own likes and dislikes, I'd forced what had worked so well for me in my life – soccer – onto hers, despite the fact that her mind was miles from any soccer field.

Instead of letting my daughter discover her own likes and dislikes, I'd forced what had worked so well for me in my life onto hers.

The very next weekend, Lindsey, too, had hung up her cleats and was perched in a saddle of an old mare named Kaluhua. Over the next decade, she eventually owned her own horse and rode her way to dozens of blue ribbons, medals, and trophies as a show jumper.

A soccer ball was my thing; a saddle was my daughter's. But it took the bright light of a BGI on that rainy day for me to finally realize it.

The Big Picture BGI

BGI's don't only refer to insights about specific instances of our own negative behavior. They can also relate to a bigger picture of how we feel about ourselves and our lives as a whole – what we've accomplished, whether or not we're happy, if we feel satisfied with our situations, our professions, our circle of friends, our families – again, all of which relate to the Me I Really Am.

Did any of you see that fun little early 1990s movie, "Singles," which chronicled the lives and loves of a group of 20- and 30-somethings living in Seattle? The quirky Janet, played by Bridget Fonda, was in love with grunged-out rocker boy Cliff (Matt Dillon), who treated her with a take-her-or-leave-her nonchalance. One of Janet's criteria for guys she dated was someone who told her "bless you" when she sneezed, and turns out one of those sneezes snapped a BGI to life for Janet in regards to her relationship with Cliff. As they hung out one day in Cliff's apartment with his burnout band, Janet purposefully sneezed twice. Instead of saying "bless you" or even *"gesundheit,"* Cliff simply passed Janet a box of tissues and told her to be careful since he had a gig coming up and didn't want to risk getting sick and losing his voice.

You could almost see the light bulb going off in Janet's head. *Wait a minute,* she said to herself. *What am I doing? I don't have to be here. I could just break up with him.* And indeed she did, at the exact moment she realized her Me I Really Am was not a groupie girlfriend who put up with such ridiculous, selfish behavior from her boyfriend.

The bright light of a BGI can illuminate at any time, whether it's someone else pointing out negative things we've said or done, or when we experience a moment of clarity, like Janet, with regards to a present situation (usually unfavorable) we face or deal with. Sometimes, we're hit with a BGI about our own lives when people around us reach a landmark or milestone in theirs, which provides a sort of measuring stick for self-reflection about our accomplishments, success, or satisfaction (or lack thereof) about our current state of affairs. For example, have you ever felt slightly wistful when a friend told you excitedly about his great new job – not because you're jealous of his achievement, but because you're secretly a little bit dissatisfied with your own professional status at the moment? All of these possibilities help us to define the

> The bright light of a BGI can illuminate at any time.

Me I Really Am by allowing us to explore and uncover what makes *us* happy, the morals and values we believe in, and ultimately what will fulfill us in our jobs, marriages, and friendships.

Regardless of how it happens, a BGI provides us with knowledge about ourselves that's often painful – but also a crucial element in the growth process. A BGI can be the first step in modifying our behavior, because it illuminates aspects of ourselves that we don't like and don't want to be reflected in the Me I Really Am. I didn't want to be a selfish, egocentric father bent on forcing his own likes and interests onto his children. Janet didn't want to be a passive doormat of a girlfriend. I'm sure you've had BGIs of your own – what kind of knowledge about yourself did they bring to light? And, more importantly, what did you do with that knowledge?

The most important aspect of a BGI is how we react to it. I certainly modified my behavior with regards to my daughter – by taking her off the soccer field and putting her atop a horse the very next weekend. Janet did, too, by leaving Cliff. A BGI is often the first critical step in bringing about change in ourselves. Once we're aware of an aspect of the Me I Really Am that we don't like, we can then begin the process of modifying our behavior.

Advice to Stick With

BGIs are a key component along the journey to self-discovery. Learn to recognize them – and understand that they will probably sting. But that's okay – because the painful insight they deliver can be a catalyst for bringing about positive changes in yourself, and consequently, in your relationships with others.

Chapter 6

The Me I Used to Be

I tend to live in the past because most of my life is there.
- Herb Caen

$\mathcal{D}$ig up that high school senior photo again. We're going to use it to help illustrate another of our concepts of self: the **Me I Used to Be.**

As we discussed earlier, change is the one thing we can count on to be permanent in life. Therefore, when we're looking at that photo, we know we're not the same person we were when it was taken two, ten, twenty years ago. We've become wiser. More confident. More successful at our jobs and with our families. Or perhaps we're more jaded. Less carefree. Less willing to take risks. We've probably changed drastically in some ways, but only a little in others. Whatever the case, the Me I Used to Be is probably a very different person than who you are now.

For some people, the Me I Used to Be is a concept of self they'd like to remain in the past. The alcoholic who's been sober for twenty years may talk about the desperate, drunken mess he was before rehab, but I don't think he wants to relapse into that state again. The young woman who's gone through an extensive full-body makeover shows off her new figure, hairstyle, and outfit in front of a television audience, but I doubt she wants to ever revert to the person in her "before" photo.

Like such "before" photos, the reminders we sometimes keep of the Me I Used to Be – the first dollar we earned in our business framed on the wall, the first trophy we won as a novice runner – can be measuring sticks indicating how far we've risen and how much we've achieved. I once knew a high-powered, well-respected executive of a utility company who started at the entry level and, rung by rung, climbed the ranks of the business. To keep a constant reminder of his humbler beginnings and his hard work throughout his journey to the top, this executive mounted and plated his original work boots, tool belt, and some of his electric tools on his office wall. The equipment sent this message to anyone who set foot in that corner office with the great view: Look where I started, and see where I am now.

Sometimes, these kinds of mementos can also be disappointing indications of how far we've fallen – perhaps the letter jacket of the All-State high school quarterback, now an overweight, disgruntled, middle-aged man whose life hasn't exactly measured up to the euphoric bliss of his high school days. This former football star can never really forget the Me I Used to Be – a standout athlete, popular with the girls, revered by the guys. He can't help but compare that glittering past with his less-than-enviable present – which is categorized by a deadbeat job, a failed marriage, and poor health. His letter jacket is a painful reminder of how far his life has fallen from the Me I Used to Be, so he keeps the jacket in the attic, where it sits gathering dust and where no one can see it.

You, Me, and the Me I Used to Be

The Me I Used to Be is a huge target for politicians. Every time elections roll around, they gather with their strategists and experts, rubbing their hands and licking their lips at the prospect of whatever speck of dirt they can dig up about their opponents' pasts. Who they dated, how long they served in the military (or if they did at all), whether or not they inhaled – nothing is off limits, no matter how long ago it took place, and how different the person in question is now. Some people call this mudslinging; I call it a perfect example of how the Me I Used to Be can be used in a negative manner.

Even if you're not running for office, I'll bet at some point in your life you've been treated as if you haven't changed or evolved from the Me I Used to Be. Like an actor who can't break out of a certain character type, sometimes we find it difficult to break out of the roles others have cast for us based on the Me I Used to Be – even though it represents an outdated role.

Sometimes we find it difficult to break out of the roles others have cast for us.

Perhaps your boss can't see past the fact that your work background is in finance, but you'd really like to get into the public relations aspect of your job. For your boss, your Me I Used to Be is a shy, reticent employee happier dealing with percentage signs than people – which is an accurate description of the person you were when you joined the company. But your boss doesn't seem to notice how much you've developed your interpersonal skills since you first began working there. If you're a young adult and you've been living on your own for years, maybe your parents still call you up three times a week and remind you to drink your milk and take your vitamins and pay your credit card bill. They're acting out of love and concern, of course, but it also seems like they just don't get it that you're no longer an irresponsible college kid who could barely wake up on time for class. Consequently, they still treat you as the Me I Used to Be, although that person is no longer in line with the capable, trustworthy adult you've grown into.

I'm sure you can think of some instances in which you've been treated – or still are being treated – according to the Me I Used to Be. It's not a good feeling, is it? But it works the other way, too. If people treat *you* that way without realizing it, there's a pretty good chance you could be doing the same thing to others as well without knowing it.

The Family Reunion (and Other Forms of Torture)

Aaaah, the family reunion. Just the thought brings up a swell of emotions, some good, some bad, depending on your family and your relationship with them. Ideally, you're thrilled about visiting with all those lovely relatives you haven't seen for years. You can't wait to dive into the tables of delicious, home-cooked food. You're looking forward to sitting around drinking lemonade and reminiscing about the good old days like the stuff of a Norman Rockwell painting.

But if your family is anything like mine, there are always one or two relatives who you hope can't make the trip, because when they're around, they sour the whole weekend. Everybody has their own version of a Cousin Norman or an Aunt Gertrude. These are the folks who, when you see them, the hair on the back of your neck raises. You cringe. You look for a tree to hide behind. Or a bathroom to duck into. Any escape from having to talk to them, because they still treat you like the snot-nosed little kid or the irresponsible teenager you used to be.

Don't you hate it when those relatives do this to you?

Much in the same way these relatives can't relate to us in terms of the person we have grown into, many of us find it difficult to let go of an outdated version of the Me I Used to Be in other people. What goes hand in hand with that is how difficult it is to let go of whatever past hurts may exist with that person. I bet there are people reading this book right now who are harboring resentment against someone else for something that happened a month, a year, even *twenty* years ago (you know who you are!). But *is it possible* that the other person, the target of the anger or resentment, has likely evolved from their Me I Used to Be – though you're still treating them as

if they haven't changed? After all, haven't you said and done things toward others you've regretted in your past? Well, if that's the case, isn't it also possible that others have said and done things toward others – like you – that they've regretted in their own pasts?

> When we hang on to the anger and resentment we feel over past hurts, we're like a ship dragging its anchor along the ocean floor. Its sails are up, but it's really not making much progress in its journey.

When we hang on to the anger and resentment we feel over past hurts, we're like a ship dragging its anchor along the ocean floor. Its sails are up, but it's really not making much progress in its journey. In the same way the ship needs to release its anchor to move forward to its destination, we need to release our anger, hurt, and resentment to move forward in our lives. And the only way to do that involves what I consider the six most important words in the English language.

The Six Most Important Words in the English Language

There's a widespread misconception out there that the most important words in the English language are "thank you" (or, if you're married, you might vote for "yes, dear"). While those phrases are crucial in our relationships, I think the most powerful words that can come out of our mouths hinge on the concept of forgiveness. For example: "I'm sorry. Will you forgive me?" and "I forgive you."

Can you remember the last time you said either of those phrases? Have you *ever* said them?

Essentially, forgiveness is the act of setting someone free from an obligation to you that is a result of their wrongdoing; it is the letting go of resentment of someone for something they've done to you. Though we may understand fully what forgiveness entails, actually granting or asking for it is difficult for many of us. In fact, according to a Gallup poll, most Americans think it's important to forgive, but in reality less than half of us actually try to do so. I think that's because the concept of forgiveness butts right up against two tricky little buggers that like to throw monkey wrenches into our interpersonal relationships – Ego and Pride. This smirking, haughty pair seems to pop up every time we think we've been wronged, shortchanged, or victimized.

Thanks to our Ego and Pride, we tend to equate forgiveness with a sign of weakness, as well as an obligation for an apology from others.

Thanks to our Ego and Pride, we tend to equate forgiveness with a sign of weakness, as well as an obligation for an apology from others. Instead of accepting responsibility for our decisions and behavior, we refuse to admit and own up to our mistakes (*It's not my fault. I didn't do anything wrong*). Instead of making a decision to heal and move on, we focus on our feelings of anger, disappointment or revenge from whatever hurt was directed toward us (*I can't believe he treated me that way! I don't deserve that kind of behavior! I refuse to speak to him unless I get an apology!*). And what happens as a result? Those feelings develop into a seething, burning grudge that can significantly affect not only the health of our relationships, but our physical health as well.

A growing body of evidence suggests just how harmful this response can be. Researchers agree that, over a period of time, the stress resulting from a grudge can be a direct threat to your health. In response to that stress, your body releases chemicals including adrenaline, noradrenaline, and cortisol, which can disrupt your immune system and set you up for hypertension and some types of cardiovascular disease, according to studies funded by A Campaign for Forgiveness Research, a nonprofit organization based in Richmond, Virginia.

> Forgiveness is not something we do for the other person. It's about us, it's letting ourselves move on.

Conversely, when we decide to forgive, we replace negative, unhealthy feelings like anger, resentment, and vengefulness with healthy ones like empathy, sympathy, and sometimes even love. Research suggests that, by fostering those positive feelings, the act of forgiveness plays a role in lowering anxiety and depression and has been linked to increases in self-esteem.

We've all heard about the family or friends of murder or rape victims who have decided to forgive the killer or rapist. *I'm not sure I could do that,* you might be thinking. *How can you forgive someone who's done something so wrong?* But those who choose this course of action understand that forgiveness is not something we do for the other person. And it's not about letting them off the hook. It's about us. It's letting ourselves move on. It's freeing ourselves from the gripping grudge, that seething anger, the deep-down tension that eats away from within. The act of forgiveness essentially means we care enough about ourselves that we recognize we have the power to change our own minds, not let someone else's past actions keep control of our current feelings.

Advice to Stick With

Some of the most dispiriting,
demeaning, and destructive sticks and stones
thrown are the result of outdated views we hold of
others, or they hold of us.

○ Recognize that people have the ability and the
right to change, grow, and develop. Realize
that you might be treating others with
respect to their Me I Used to Be.
○ Take stock of the grudges you
may be holding. Drop them.
○ Make the "I'm sorry – will you forgive
me?" or "I forgive you" phrases part
of your vocabulary.

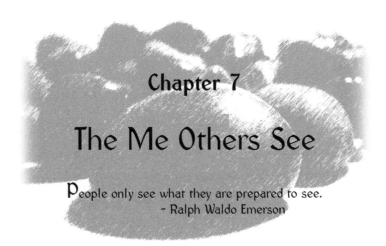

Chapter 7

The Me Others See

People only see what they are prepared to see.
- Ralph Waldo Emerson

*R*ose-colored glasses. A wide-angle lens. Beer goggles (that got your attention, didn't it, especially you college-age readers?). Literal or figurative, what do these things have in common?

They change they way we see things. They alter our perception. If someone views the world through rose-colored glasses, that person is considered an optimist because he or she tends to see life through a rosy, cheerful glow. A wide-angle lens lets the photographer capture much more of the scene than a normal lens, enabling him to take one of those amazing panoramic-style shots. And the infamous beer goggles – you young party animal types know all too well what they are, right? If the poor bloke at the Irish pub has had so many pints that, at last call, he's sweet-talking the moose head hanging on the wall, he's definitely wearing beer goggles.

> Each of us has our own set of filters.

Whatever the setting, all of these things work as filters by altering our perspective on the world around us. Much in the same way, each of us has our own set of filters as a a human being: a distinct view of the world and the people in it that results from our individual life experiences, personalities, opinions, ideas, and tastes.

Let's eavesdrop on the dinnertime conversation of a typical family one evening, where the topic of discussion is one of today's most well-known pop icons: Britney Spears. The mother, who's rather conservative, might use the adjectives "provocative," "tasteless," and "disgraceful" to describe Britney. Her pre-teen daughter might say, "talented," "beautiful," and "cool." The older daughter, who's more of a Grateful Dead fan, would probably describe Britney as, "over-rated," "annoying," and "tone-deaf." The teenage son (and maybe even his father, though he probably wouldn't admit it at the dinner table) might use, "hot," "hot," and "hot."

The adjective choices of this family in describing Britney are all over the board because the people who selected them are different ages and sexes, with varying interests, likes, and dislikes. But even for individuals with very similar demographics – age, socioeconomic backgrounds, or occupations – filters play a significant role. I've been using the same exercise in my presentations (with me as the "celebrity") for more than a decade. *Not once* – even in the most homogenous of groups, such as an audience of all-female, middle-aged churchgoers – have any two people used the same three adjectives to describe me. Again, that's because no two people have identical life experiences.

Filters on the Street

Let's look at another example. A cop is called to the scene of a wreck where two cars have wrapped themselves around each other, and the drivers, who aren't hurt, are engaged in a screaming match about whose fault it was. The cop pulls aside three eyewitnesses: a car mechanic, an engineer, and a mother of four. Here are the responses the cop received when he asked each person what happened:

Car mechanic: Well, the Honda Accord – looks like a '91 or '92 model – was making a left, and then the Chevy Blazer – I'm guessing it's the new '05 version – slammed right into it while trying to go straight through the light. Damage to both appears pretty bad – there's some nasty stuff going on internally in the Blazer from the likes of that smoke, and the Accord's driver's side door will need a complete replacement. Looks like they'll need a good mechanic. Here's my card!

Engineer: The four-door red vehicle appeared to be making a 90-degree turn, while the two-door sport-utility vehicle was continuing straight at about forty miles per hour. Judging by the length of the skid marks, the sport-utility vehicle failed to apply enough brake pressure in time to avoid a collision, but the other car, judging by its angle afterward, was surely going through that yellow light to try to make it before it changed red.

Mother of four: Well, the red car was going pretty fast, and it was making a left-hand turn when the SUV slammed into it. The sound of the crash was just awful. I just thank goodness nobody was hurt, and there were no kids in the cars.

Same cars, same wreck, same scenario – but different eyewitnesses, and consequently very different perspectives of it.

Faulty Filters

By now, you should have a pretty good grip on the concept of filters. Understanding filters is vital in understanding the next Me: the **Me Others See.**

Defining the Me Others See is contingent upon recognizing and understanding the unique set of filters each person has, which inevitably affect his perception of others. You need at least a basic amount of insight into the other person to begin to understand the Me Others See. The better you get to know a person, the better you'll understand how they perceive you.

But often, we have no clue whatsoever about the Me Others See.

Imagine yourself as a third-grade teacher. For eight hours a day, five days a week, your focus is the intellectual and social development of twenty-five eight- and nine-year-olds. Most of the time, you love your job, but there is one boy in your class – we'll call him Damien – who tests your patience, resolve, and dedication as an educator every day. Damien screams at you with some very colorful word choices. He blatantly refuses to complete assignments. He's even tried to hit you a couple of times. Any chance he gets, Damien pits himself against you. Despite your best efforts at communication and understanding, none of your strategies seem to work with this unruly demon of a child.

> The better you get to know a person, the better you'll understand how they perceive you.

One day, you're called out of class to the principal's office, where you find a distraught social worker clutching a thick case file. She begins to pull out paper after paper documenting every imaginable abuse – verbal, emotional, physical, sexual – that has happened to one particular child in foster homes he has been placed in over the years. Somehow, the file got lost in the enormous shuffle of paperwork the social services agency deals with.

The file is Damien's.

You eventually head back to the classroom, shaken, but enlightened. You now understand that as soon as Damien steps into your classroom every day, his mind clicks into survival mode at the sight of you – adult: *attack and defend, or be hurt.* In Damien's eyes, the Me Others See is not a wise teacher, a respected authority figure, or a trusted elder. He simply sees you as an adult – and nearly every adult he has encountered in his young life has hurt him. With respect to you, this is a faulty filter that Damien has.

When you re-enter that classroom after your meeting, is Damien the same little boy? Yes. Are you the same teacher? No. Because now, you see Damien through a new filter – and that filter enables you to begin to change the Me Others See for Damien. You're going to bend over backwards trying to prove to him that all adults aren't dangerous, life-threatening figures. You're going to be more patient, understanding, and empathetic. In other words, you're going to modify your behavior to change Damien's current perception of the Me Others See, so he eventually will view you as the wise teacher, respected authority figure,

Everyone has a story.

and trusted elder that you are. Ideally, at least by the end of the school year, your efforts will pay off and Damien will see you through a new filter of his own as well.

Figuring Out Our Filters

Filters apply to every scenario in our lives, from the classroom to the boardroom. From the conference table to the kitchen table. From the playing field to the dating field. Only after we make an effort to become aware of our own filters and the filters through which others see us can we develop an accurate picture of the Me Others See. From there, we have a much better understanding of the motivations behind others' behavior and actions toward us, whether they're positive or negative.

And when we have a grasp of the filters of others, we can begin to modify our behavior to help fix whatever faulty filters might exist. In effect, we create new filters through which others can see a newer, more accurate picture of who we really are.

As my wife likes to say, everyone has a story. Each of us has a road we've walked down. Our individual journey of events, circumstances, and unique experiences – both good and bad – shapes our outlook on life and how we view and relate to each other. Having some insight into those personal landscapes – in other words, what has helped create others' filters – can help unlock a much higher potential for effective communication and stronger relationships.

> It's up to us to change our behaviors or actions when others' faulty filters are impeding communication.

When we can determine where a faulty filter is impeding our interactions, we can then begin to modify our own behavior to help others break through their inaccurate perception of us. Like the teacher that day: Once she realized the Me Others See from Damien's perspective was inaccurate, it was her responsibility to modify her own behavior to help Damien replace his faulty filter. The one he'd developed through all his horrible experiences in his home life was not applicable in this classroom, and the teacher bent over backwards to help him see her in a different light. The same is true for us. When we come across Damiens in our own lives, it's up to us to change our behaviors or actions when their faulty filters are impeding communication.

Advice to Stick With

○ Be aware of the unique set of filters each of us possesses. No two people are exactly the same. No two sets of filters can be the same either. Ultimately, people will see things differently.

○ The better you know someone, the more you understand how they see the world – and how they see you.

○ When friction arises, try to figure out the filters others might have in the situation. Be prepared to modify your own behavior to help fix faulty filters, if they exist.

Chapter 8

The Me I Try to Project

Study to be what you wish to seem.
- John Bate

Shakespeare had it right: All the world is a stage. In one way or another, we're all actors in various aspects of our lives. We're constantly trying to project ourselves in a certain light to the world around us. Of all of our concepts of self, the **Me I Try to Project** gets the most practice. It's always on display. It's who we want others to see.

> We're constantly trying to project ourselves in a certain light to the world around us.

Think about the first-time teacher on her very first day of class. She's probably scared to death standing there in front of all those expectant new faces, but she's trying to convey the opposite: that she's a confident, in-control authority figure. That she rules the roost of this classroom. That her mere presence commands respect and attention.

It's the same thing for the waitress in a fancy restaurant who's great at her job, but doesn't know too much about the wine list. She's got a basic understanding of it, of course, but she certainly could learn a lot more. Still, she knows her tips will reflect a directly proportional relationship to how well she can describe and sell these wines to her customers – so she's playing up every aspect of the knowledge she does have. She's describing that Merlot as a wonderful vintage, this Chardonnay as crisp and refreshing, and that Bordeaux as an exquisite full-flavor experience. She's not lying, but the Me she's trying to project is a waitress so well-versed with those wines that she could be a sommelier.

Let's not forget athletes, either. A popular phrase in today's sports-speak is the "game face" – the image of toughness, of readiness, of preparation athletes try to convey despite the fact that they might have a horde of butterflies swarming around in their stomach before the first whistle. This is the same image you see of those athletes in sports drink or shoe commercials, their sweat-drenched faces hardened into stone-cold expressions, their eyes boring through you with an intensity that says, *I'm a warrior. I'm a machine. I'm unbeatable.*

For me, the Me I Try to Project at church is significantly less intense, but I can count on it popping up every once in a while. Life in the Weber household is pretty laid back, but when Sunday mornings roll around we sometimes turn into crazed lunatics trying to get to church on time.

It's a little easier now that both of my children are in their teens and can pretty much take care of themselves. But it wasn't always that way. Let me share with you perhaps one of the most infamous episodes in our family history – and a humbling illustration of the Me I Try to Project.

8:11 a.m. Mmmmmm, I slept so well last night . . . I must have been so out of it I didn't even hear the alarm . . . . *Alarm?!?* As in alarm for church – the one with 9 a.m. service? The one that's forty-five minutes away? *"TINA-WAKE-UP-WAKE-UP! WE'RE-GOING-TO-BE-LATE-*

YOU-GET-DRESSED-I'LL-GET-THE-KIDS-READY-HURRY-LET'S-GO-GET-UP!"
Aaah, nothing like the quiet calm of a lazy Sunday morning.

8:13 a.m. Mad dash down the hall to my daughter's room, where my then-five-year-old Lindsey is sleeping like a little angel. I coax her limp body out of bed, over to the closet and into the first dress I can find – which has no less than ninety-seven buttons down the front. *Great choice, Dave,* I think as I fumble with the last few blasted little pieces of plastic – not only have I just lost ten minutes, now I've got to bandage my blistered fingers from all those *&^%$ buttons. But no time to think about that. I've got to get Logan dressed now, too – a task I'm much more familiar with. In a shirt-pants-shoes-socks-tornado, my three-year-old son is dressed.

8:25 a.m. Mad dash back down the hall to the master bathroom, where Tina is putting the final touches on her makeup. I jostle for mirror space, nearly causing her to impale her eye with the mascara wand – *"Sorry, honey, gotta get a quick shave in"* – and manage to nick myself at least ten times in two minutes. (At least my inflamed skin hides those pillow marks zigzagging across my face.)

8:27 a.m. As I scramble for a tie, I hear a menacing bellow from down the hall, thinking maybe there *is* a monster living underneath Lindsey's bed. Mad dash back to her room. Lindsey still looks half-asleep, but Tina looks half-human, her face contorted with consternation. I half-expect her head to start spinning around on her neck. *"LOOK . . . . AT . . . YOUR . . . DAUGHTER!"* she snarls, thrusting

Lindsey at me like a puppet. "What?" I ask, admiring my speedy handiwork with those maddening buttons. *"YOU... DRESSED ... HER .... BACKWARDS!"* Ooops ... I'm a guy, for goodness' sake, how was I supposed to know those cursed buttons go down the back? No way am I going to let all that hard work go to waste, though. I grab Lindsey, yank the dress over head, flip it around, stuff it over back down over her head, and yank out her arms – this time, with those *&^@! buttons in the back.

8:31 a.m. Mad dash to the car, where Lindsey and Logan pile into the backseat. I mash the accelerator to the floor like a race-car driver on the last lap of the Indy 500.

8:35 a.m. The kids begin to bicker. My blood begins to boil. *"YOU TWO CUT IT OUT OR I'LL PULL THIS CAR OVER SO FAST ..."* Actually, I won't – I'm already going fast enough to break the sound barrier; pulling over at this point could have dire consequences.

8:47 a.m. Still twenty miles away. Please dear Lord, we're on our way to Your House – please help me out and keep the cops out of my way, can You?

8:59 a.m. We screech into the church parking lot, tires squealing, dust churning. Lindsey and Logan are still fussing, Tina is still fuming about being late, my face is still full of little bits of toilet paper stuck to my shaving wounds and, in short, *I am one giant nerve.* We pile out of the car, Logan hits Lindsey, and my blood pressure hits an all-time high: *"YOU TWO STOP FIGHTING RIGHT THIS INSTANT OR I'LL – "* I'm cut off by a friend of mine walking into the church with his family. He waves and asks, "Good morning, Dave, how are you today?" "PRAISE the Lord, I am doing fantastic on this GLORI-OUS day the Lord has made! How are you, brother?"

And there you have the Me I Try to Project on Sunday mornings: a righteous, grateful, churchgoing individual attending service with his beloved, precious family – nearly the opposite of the frazzled, impious, crazed human being I often am.

Why We Take the Stage

In scenarios where we think we may be judged or categorized or viewed a certain way, the Me I Try to Project can be a powerful motivator of our behavior. It often takes center stage over our other concepts of self as we try to behave in a certain way in front of certain people in certain situations. Consequently, the Me I Try to Project often has several variations. For example, the Me I Try to Project in the church parking lot looks nothing like the Me I Try to Project when I'm presenting in front of an audience of five hundred executives at a conference. The Me I Try to Project as the president of my business is a completely different Me I Try to Project as a father.

> The Me I Try to Project often takes center stage over our other concepts of self.

Many times, the Me I Try to Project represents a healthy and necessary adaptation of our behavior, especially in authority positions. Let's go back to that brand-new kindergarten teacher on the first day of class. Do you think she'll be able to survive a year with a group of rambunctious five-year-olds who could walk all over her the first day of class because they could sense how nervous and insecure she felt? Certainly not. So she projects that she's calm, confident, and in control – a teacher who will *not* be treated as a doormat for the rest of the year.

In situations like this – where our insecurity stems from our lack of knowledge, experience, or understanding of something – we sometimes hear the phrase "Fake it 'til you make it." Especially in work or occupational environments, this advice represents a useful application of the Me I Try to Project. It encourages us to take the mindset that, although we might not know what we're doing at the moment, we will, at some point "make it." The implied meaning is that whatever we're trying to "fake" for the time being – whether it be proficiency in a new position, confidence during an interview, or background about a product line – will get us through until we can learn those things for real.

But there are other times when that strategy doesn't quite work, especially where emotions are involved. Don't we all know someone who's been through a difficult time in his life, perhaps following a divorce or the loss of a job, but refuses to let his true feelings show for fear of being seen as weak or unable to deal with adversity? Instead of leaning on others to help them make it through those trying times, people like this keep a stone-cold façade on the Me I Try to Project. As a result, they often have an even more difficult time overcoming their problems because they're keeping them locked up inside.

Self-esteem issues are also at the heart of the Me I Try to Project for another class of individuals: the braggarts.

You know the type: They never miss the chance to tell you about their top-of-the-line sports car, which they can afford because of their six-figure salary, which resulted from a promotion they received for landing that oh-so-important account. These folks are tooting their own horns so loudly that any shred of the real person lying underneath all those embellishments is lost in the noise. That's because, deep down, they don't think that person – the Me I Really Am – warrants much attention, so they have to spice everything up with a flashy, Rolex-wearing, five-foot-fish-catching Me I Try to Project.

Though we shift through different variations of the Me I Try to Project depending on the situation, we are almost always trying to make sure it lines up with the Me Others See. Sometimes it does, sometimes it doesn't; it depends on the filters we talked about earlier. But you can be sure that if an executive at a busy advertising agency is trying to project himself as a genius at his job – on top of trends in the advertising world, well-versed about his client's needs – you can bet that's the same image he's hoping everyone around him sees.

> As our relationships with others grow, the Me I Try to Project becomes less of a factor in determining our behavior.

Removing the Mask

As our relationships with others grow, the Me I Try to Project becomes less of a factor in determining our behavior because we're more comfortable with that person – and less concerned about always being on stage, projecting ourselves as the model of perfection. We're more trusting. Less suspicious of judgment or criticism. More open to letting our true self – the Me I Really Am – shine through, even if that Me isn't a model of perfection. So the Me I Try to Project slowly moves off center stage and takes a spot backstage, allowing other Me's to take the lead role for a change.

Advice to Stick With

○ Take the bamboo tube away and broaden your view: Try to find out why you're trying to project yourself as something you may not be. Is it a healthy response? Does it really matter what others think of you in certain situations?

○ When necessary, "Fake it 'til you make it."

○ Recognize when to drop the act.

Chapter 9

The Me Others Try to Make Me

Keep away from people who try to belittle your ambitions. Small people always do that, but the really great make you feel like you, too, can become great.
- Mark Twain

$\mathcal{M}$uch in the same way we're trying to project ourselves in a certain light to others, they're trying to project their opinions, values, and morals onto us – and in doing so, we have the **Me Others Try to Make Me.** It could also be called the Me Others Try to Mold Me Into, or the Me Others Try to Shape Me Into, or as one of my workshop participants once said, the "Me My Husband Wants Me to Be." However you want to look at it, this concept of self has a bit of a negative connotation.

We bristle a little when we think about others trying to change us, don't we? If people are trying to make us into something or someone else, it means they think there's something wrong with us just as we are, right? If we read between the lines, what those others are saying through their actions is that we're in some way flawed, right?

> We bristle a little when we think about others trying to change us.

To answer these questions, it's crucial to determine *why* people are trying to change us – because the answer determines the degree to which we pursue or resist this concept of self. Are they acting out of love, respect, and care for us – because they sincerely want to see us achieve our best potential and rise to all that we can become? Are they behaving out of personal gain, manipulating us for their own interests, trying to make us conform to some standard, ideal, or moral that doesn't fall in line with those of our own? Or is your behavior something they hope to help change because it affects them in a negative way? These are crucial questions to address, because the answers determine the degree to which we pursue or reject becoming this Me.

Who in your life is trying to mold you or make you into something you aren't? Your spouse? Your boss? Your parents? Your significant other? Your teacher? Your mother-in-law? And, on the flip side, who might you be trying to change? Your spouse? Your employees? Your children? Your significant other? Your students? Your mother-in-law?

When We Could Use a Little Molding

When I was a youngster in elementary school, still being called Shrimpus by my classmates, my father's routine after coming home from the office was like clockwork. He'd climb into his armchair, snap open the newspaper, and light up a cigarette. While my younger brother and I were playing on the floor a few feet away, Dad buried himself in the expanse of gray newsprint. But his presence infiltrated the room through the clouds and columns of smoke that continuously rose from behind the pages.

One afternoon, I climbed onto his lap, pushed away the sports section with a loud crackle, and asked him a question that, in the long run, perhaps saved his life. "Daddy," I asked, coughing a little as he exhaled, "why do you want to die?"

My father, a fairly outspoken and verbose man, was speechless. Seems that day in school I'd learned about smoking and its dangers, including the gravest of those. So in my young mind, I equated the cigarettes my father puffed every day with dying, and my point-blank questioning pretty much summed up where he was headed with the habit. From that day on, my father found that he could no longer light up without hearing my simple inquiry echo in his mind.

Gradually, his behavior changed. He stood around in our garage in the dead of the brutal Cape Cod winter, barely getting in a few drags through his clattering teeth, realizing that those cigarettes were about to be the cause of death not by lung disease – but by frostbite. Eventually, he quit smoking. Today he's sixty-six and he can still kick my tail around a racquetball court.

"Daddy," I asked, "why do you want to die?"

Of course, I had no clue about it at the time, but I was helping shape the Me Others Try to Make Me for my father. As he'll tell you today, I think he's still around because of what I asked him that day in the armchair after school.

Bad Habits and Beyond

Of course, the situation with my father involved no psychoanalysis on my part in exposing my father's deadly addiction for what it was. In similar scenarios when dire health consequences are a factor, the Me Others Try to Make Me can be a crucial catalyst for change. Certainly, negative habits like smoking, drinking, and gambling can be highly detrimental to our health. And if we're constantly doing those things, it's natural that the Me Others Try to Make Me will get lots of attention as our loved ones try to help us overcome our addictions to become physically healthier individuals.

But although the health of our relationships is a little different than our physical health, it's equally deserving of our attention. Consequently, the Me Others Try to Make Me often encompasses concepts of self that relate not just to the physical aspects of ourselves and others – encouraging loved ones to quit smoking, lose weight, or dress better, for example – but also to more psychological aspects. Perhaps the Me Others Try to Make Me is a father who spends more time with his children. Or a friend who isn't so critical. Or a spouse who is more affectionate. I mentioned this before, but it bears repeating: It's crucial that we know why these people are trying to change us, because the answer determines the degree to which we pursue or reject this Me.

> Though we may hesitate when we think about others trying to change us, it's not always a negative thing.

In the previous examples, it's safe to say the people influencing the Me Others Try to Make Me (the children who want to spend more time with their father; the person who wants her friend to cut back on her criticism; the spouse who wants her husband to demonstrate more affection) are acting not out of manipulative interest. In these cases, the Me Others Try to Make Me is a better Me. Though we may hesitate when we think about others trying to change us, it's not always a negative thing.

Keep in mind that it's not really in our psychological makeup to solicit feedback from others about how we need to make changes in ourselves. But if we can succeed in this, the benefits for our relationships can be immeasurable.

So, if we can feel the push and pull of the Me Others Try to Make Me, and we determine the people behind that Me and our relationships with them are important enough for us to consider the change they want, how do we go about implementing it?

A good way to start is by asking a simple question.

One Crucial Question

What is the one thing you wish I would start/stop (pick one) doing immediately?

Sounds like such a simple inquiry, but before you ask it, consider if you're brave enough to hear an honest answer, and courageous enough to act upon that answer.

This question – and your response to it – can be a phenomenal catalyst in moving closer toward koinonia with whoever you ask it. At first, it may feel unnatural. After all, as I earlier mentioned, it's not really in our psychological makeup to solicit feedback from others. We're much better at telling people how they should act, behave, or change instead of listening to similar input directed at us.

But lay that question out there, and just watch the surprise, smile, or shock spread across the other person's face. Whatever the form, I guarantee you'll get a reaction. Simply by asking the question, you've demonstrated a conscious effort in establishing koinonia by considering the other person's input, feelings, and needs – reflected by whatever it is you *aren't* doing that they want you to start, or whatever it is you *are* doing that they wish you'd stop. If we're trying to move forward on the koinonia continuum with others, regardless of the type of relationship, it's in our best interest to find out what those things are.

The next step is even more crucial: actually acting on whatever the answer is. For example, if you ask the start/stop question to your wife and the answer is something along the lines of, *"I'd like you to start coming home earlier so we can have dinner together as a family,"* and you continue spending long hours at the office and missing dinner, what message are you sending? You're basically communicating that your wife and family's desires and needs are less important than your finishing a report, sending out that last e-mail, or any number of other details associated with your job.

After my daughter Lindsey hung up her cleats and hopped on a saddle, our relationship took a quantum leap on the koinonia continuum when, one night while I tucked her in, I asked her the above crucial question: "What is the one thing you wish I would start doing immediately?"

She didn't hesitate for a second in answering. "Daddy, I wish you'd come watch me ride my horse sometimes."

My traveling and speaking schedule made it extremely difficult for me to get out to the stables during the week. That left the weekend – which was already pretty full with my Sunday school teaching commitments, our family's church activities, weekend chores, and errands. I had to make a decision: watch my daughter ride during her lesson on Saturday morning, or continue preparing for my Sunday school classes on Saturday. At first, I tried rearranging things to plan my lesson during the week. But I'm most productive on projects by devoting large chunks of time to them, instead of breaking them up into little pieces. And I just couldn't find a several-hour pocket of available time during the week to plan my Sunday school lessons.

In the end, I decided to give up my teaching commitments. Because, if I had continued preparing for the class, what message would it have sent to my daughter? That a roomful of other kids were more important to me than spending time with her. Giving up the class was a difficult decision, of course, but in the end it was one I was glad I made after seeing Lindsey's delight when I came to watch her Saturday riding lessons. And her request wasn't unreasonable – after all, since I had been an avid (and often crazed) attendee at her Saturday soccer games, why couldn't I use that time to watch her ride her horse instead? Today, I'm proud to say Lindsey and I have a relationship that's exceptionally high on the koinonia continuum. I believe quality time we spent together when she was young, like Saturday mornings at the stables, are a large part of the reason why.

> If I had continued preparing for the class, what message would it have sent to my daughter?

But had Lindsey answered my question with something like, "Daddy, I want you to start coming to the stables to watch *all* of my lessons," that would have been an entirely different – and unfeasible – demand of my time. Consequently, I would have been unable, and unwilling, to honor her request.

These concepts apply to any relationship when we're talking about adapting and changing behaviors. Reasonableness, compromise, and flexibility play a key role when considering the Me Others Try to Make Me, as well as awareness on both sides about the limits of change.

Blind Spots

We've already talked about BGI's, which are blinding glimpses of insight. A closely related concept is a blind spot. Those of us with driver's licenses know what the conventional definition of a blind spot is: an area alongside the car that escapes the scope of the car's side mirrors enough so we can't see other vehicles when they pass through that area. When we're driving, blind spots can be dangerous. We always have to be on the lookout for other cars that might be passing through them.

In a non-driving context, blind spots also refer to aspects of ourselves that we can't see – and they can be hazardous to the health of our relationships. Our blind spots escape our own vision, but other people, especially spouses, best friends, parents, and even our co-workers, can often see with 20/20 clarity into them. Other times, BGI situations like the one I had on Lindsey's rainy game day shine light into our blind spots. We can also become aware of our blind spots by asking the start/stop question – "What is the one thing you wish I would start/stop doing?" – and then listening carefully to the answer. Many times, the response will illuminate an aspect of ourselves that we were unable to see but are willing to change.

Here's another way to look at it. The answer to the start/stop question will often lead us to a BGI, which will then illuminate a blind spot into ourselves. And once we can see into that blind spot, we can take the necessary steps to change our behavior.

Advice to Stick With

○ Recognize that the Me Others Try to Make Me can be a very positive influence on your life.
○ Take a hard look at the motivations of others. Why are people trying to make you into something different? On the flip side, how you might be trying to make other people conform to your ideas of what they should be?
○ Recognize that there is a difference in trying to change a behavior and trying to change a person.

Chapter 10

The Me I Want to Be

There is only one corner of the universe you can be certain of improving, and that's your own self.
– Aldous Huxley

*E*verybody – you, me, the butcher, the baker, the candlestick maker – embodies some form of the **Me I Want to Be.** The Me I Want to Be reflects our highest goals, our loftiest ideals, and our brightest dreams. It embodies our highest potential as an individual. It's the person we aspire to be. We want to be a better parent. A more loving spouse. A more effective manager.

Of course, there are unrealistic variations of the Me I Want to Be. Often, these versions embody characteristics that are usually out of reach and superficial, often based on looks, talents, or material wealth. For example, I would love to be a six-foot, muscle-rippled Greek god who could fire a fastball at a hundred miles an hour while earning my eight-figure salary over the next year. But unless I give up my day job to become an iron-pumping gym rat and undergo the first growth spurt ever documented for a forty-something man, I'm painfully aware that specific version is a highly unlikely – and unattainable – image for me.

> The Me I Want to Be reflects our highest goals, our loftiest ideals, and our brightest dreams. It's the person we aspire to be.

So instead of wasting our time and energy on an ideal we're not likely to reach, let's focus on the attainable, achievable Me I Want to Be. It's a much healthier approach.

There are volumes of material out there related to this concept of self. They range from topics like goal-setting to achieving your highest potential to discovering your purpose and place in life. Books, research studies, seminars, and even religions explore the subject in depth. Their scope can include personality tests, plenty of reflection on your past, and lots of Freudian-speak. If you're interested, I encourage you to dig in with gusto. At the very least, you're bound to learn a thing or two about yourself. But for the purposes of this book, we're going to continue on a simpler path in uncovering and understanding the Me I Want to Be.

Who *Isn't* This Me?

For some of us, trying to define or articulate the Me I Want to Be is a little overwhelming. Figuring out the values, characteristics, and goals we envision for ourselves is no easy task. They are concepts that constantly evolve throughout our lives as our outlooks, knowledge, and opinions shift and develop. So here's a little secret that help can jump-start the process.

> Sometimes, it's easier to define something by looking at its opposite.

Sometimes, it's easier to define something by looking at its opposite. Therefore, it can be easier to identify qualities, traits, or characteristics that you *don't* want to embody: *"I* don't *want to be an overbearing manager or parent";* *"I* don't *want to feel exhausted all the time"; "I* don't *want to feel disrespected or overlooked in my work environment."* In doing so, you help to clarify the Me I Want to Be. Similar to the process of elimination, this approach can be an effective tool in helping us uncover what really defines us. By identifying ourselves in terms of what we don't want to be, we can often more easily determine the characteristics or attributes we *do* want to strive for.

This Year, I Resolve to . . .

Let's look at this Me another way. Not all of us believe in New Year's resolutions (I realize it's become rather trendy these days to brush off the tradition) but everyone understands the premise. The essence of these resolutions boils down to self-improvement: *"I want to work out more and eat healthier so I can lose fifteen pounds and look great in my bathing suit." "I'll practice the piano for an hour every day so I'll really shine at my recital." "I'll focus on spending more time with my kids and out of the office."*

These resolutions are really just offshoots of our life goals, aren't they? In other words, they help us define the Me I Want to Be in various aspects of our lives, whether it's achieving a stronger, more fit physique, honing our skills at an instrument or sport, or becoming a more involved parent. The resolutions represent tangible results of qualities embodied by the Me I Want to Be. For example, if your goal is to work out more and eat better, your Me I Want to Be in achieving that goal could be described as a healthy, self-respecting individual who values herself enough to take the best possible care of herself. If your goal is to really rock at your recital, your Me I Want to Be would likely be a talented, creative musician. If you envision spending more time with your children, your Me I Want to Be is probably an attentive, devoted father.

But other than during the annual rush of the holiday season with January 1 just around the corner, do you honestly take the time to think about this very powerful concept of self? Do you know what the Me I Want to Be looks like? Who is your Me I Want to Be as a parent? As a spouse? As a team member in your company? As a third baseman for your recreational softball team? As a daughter? As a boyfriend? Have you thought about who those people are, what characteristics they embody, and how you can move closer to becoming them?

Lost Planes and Off-Course Ships

When we don't have a clear picture of the Me I Want to Be, it's impossible to gauge our progress in becoming that person. It's like the story about the pilot who comes over the airplane's loudspeaker and says, "The good news, folks, is that we've got a strong tailwind. The bad news is, we're lost." Or, as Greek philosopher Socrates once said, "The ship that has not set its course finds no wind favorable." Like that lost plane or ship sailing astray, if we don't know where we're headed in our personal growth, how will we know if we ever get there, even with the help of a strong wind?

Remember *Alice in Wonderland?* Lewis Carroll's classic, later made into a Disney movie, addressed some timeless lessons through Alice's wild journey through a mystical, make-believe world. One of the most poignant of those lessons was a subtle message about knowing where you're headed in life. When Alice found herself at a fork in the road, she walked up to the Cheshire Cat, perched jauntily in a tree, to ask for help. Their conversation went something like this:

"Which way, please, ought I to go from here?" Alice asked the cat.

"That depends a good deal on where you want to get to," replied the cat, his signature grin stretched across his face.

"I don't much care where – " said Alice.

"Then it doesn't matter which way you go," said the cat.

" – so long as I get somewhere," Alice added.

"Oh, you're sure to do that," continued the cat, "if only you walk long enough."

Like Alice, many of us walk through our own life journey without knowing where we want to go, and consequently, which path to take to get there. Without even realizing it, we drift through on a rudderless course without much aim, target, or direction about where we want to go, or why.

Does this describe you?

The Good in Goal-Setting

As I've mentioned before, the focus of this book isn't about how to define and achieve your goals – I'll leave that to other experts who have far more to say about the matter. Nor will I list pages of hard facts and in-depth research showing the benefits of goal setting and how it can change your life. Instead, I'll emphasize that it's been well-documented that those who set goals consistently achieve higher in corporate, academic, and personal growth environments. Whether we want to climb a rung on the corporate ladder, learn how to play the guitar, or get in shape to run a marathon, determining and assessing our goals provides us with systematic

We can set goals for the type of person we'd like to become.

evidence of all the great things we're capable of. In essence, goals are a motivator for and a measuring stick of our potential and the success we can achieve.

Just as we set goals for what we'd like to accomplish, we can also set them for the type of person we'd like to become. In the same way identifying and clarifying our goals is the first step in achieving them, identifying and clarifying ourselves with respect to the Me I Want to Be is the first step in becoming this Me. The degree to which we give this concept of self clarity is the degree to which we will become or begin moving toward it.

> The better you crystallize the Me I Want to Be, the greater chance you have of achieving or becoming this Me.

In other words, the better you crystallize the Me I Want to Be, the greater chance you have of achieving or becoming this Me. But if you don't know who this Me is, how will you ever know if that's who you're moving toward becoming?

For example, what is your Me I Want to Be when conflict arises at work? Do you *want* to be a person who loses his temper, shouts obscenities, and then storms out of the conference room, slamming the door loudly? Or an employee who bottles up her concerns while secretly spreading a kind of "Us Versus Them" mentality among fellow co-workers and gunning for an Office Showdown at the water cooler?

While these kind of actions might be your behavior, I'd bet they aren't an accurate reflection of your Me I Want to Be – your highest goals, loftiest ideals, and brightest aspirations for yourself as an employee or team member. Instead, it's behavior more like that of a petulant preschooler, not a competent professional in Corporate America.

Or, on the opposite end of the spectrum, is your Me I Want to Be the kind of employee who's emotionally mature enough to consider all sides of an issue? One who can calmly analyze all viewpoints in a rational manner to help the team reach the best decision? I'm guessing this is much more along the lines of the expectations and goals you have for yourself – your Me I Want to Be – in a work environment. However, when door-slamming, obscenity-shouting, and stealthy back-stabbing is the behavior we choose, we're heading in the exact opposite direction of that Me.

We're all guilty of this at times: behaving in ways that are not consistent with our Me I Want to Be. My thirteen-year-old son, Logan, who's an extremely talented golfer, wants to one day qualify for the PGA tour. But, at one point, he didn't always put in the amount of practice time on the course he knew he needed to in order to reach his goal. In my own life trajectory, the Me I Want to Be is one of the top professional speakers in the United States, a widely respected, well-known individual who presents before audiences of thousands of rapt listeners. But there are times, although rare, when I don't put forth the incredible amount of nonstop energy, research, and preparation it takes to reach that level – effort that's exactly in line with the Me I Want to Be as a speaker, and effort that I admittedly need to invest *every single time* I give a presentation.

> We're all guilty of this at times: behaving in ways that are not consistent with our Me I Want to Be.

If you have crystallized the Me I Want to Be – whether it's as an employee, manager, friend, parent, daughter, or student – it's much easier to realize when you're behaving in ways that don't reflect this concept of self. I know where I want to be as a speaker one day, so it's pretty obvious when I'm not behaving in ways that will get me there. Similarly, Logan knows where he wants to be as a golfer, and he's well aware when he's not doing what it takes to reach that level.

This recognition is pivotal in changing our behavior so that it *does* reflect the Me I Want to Be. And when we change our behavior to reflect that Me, we put ourselves back on track to reach our highest potential. It doesn't happen often, but when I find myself lacking my usual spark while giving a presentation, I remind myself of my goals as a professional speaker – and that inevitably boosts my energy level back up to 150 percent. Once Logan truly began to crystallize his Me I Want to Be as a professional golfer, he began to change his practice habits. He now has one of the most dedicated work ethics I've seen in a thirteen-year-old.

When we align our behavior with the Me I Want to Be, we do more than just maximize our own potential. We also, as I'll explain more later, lay down the groundwork to unlock one of the most powerful elements of effective communication.

Advice to Stick With

The Me I Want to Be reflects your
highest goals, dreams, and aspirations.

○ Analyze the Me I Want to Be in your different
roles as a person: What is your Me I Want to
Be as a parent? An employee? A spouse?
A friend? A son or daughter?

○ Put pen to paper with adjectives, goals, objectives,
and behaviors that define your Me I Want to Be. The
degree to which you define it is the degree to which
you'll become it.

○ Sometimes it helps to work backwards. Identify
characteristics, qualities, and behaviors you don't want
to embody to help you figure out those you do.

○ When your behavior, words, or attitudes
do not line up with your Me I Want to Be, it's
time to change your behavior, words,
and attitudes.

Chapter 11

The Logjam of Me's

Our background and circumstances may influence who we are, but we are responsible for who we will become.
- Unknown

*I*t's a little odd to think about all those different concepts of self running around inside us, isn't it? When we think about them individually, it's not quite so overwhelming. Often, we tend to categorize our Seven Me's chronologically. We reflect on our pasts – the Me I Used to Be – and compare them to the person we've evolved into, which is reflected in different ways by the Me I Really Am, the Me I Think I Am, the Me Others See, the Me Others Try to Make Me, and the Me I Try to Project. And we envision our goals, our future, and consequently, our place and role in both – all of which encompass the Me I Want to Be.

But we need to remember that each concept of self is always present in each of us. Kind of like a rowdy group of kindergartners, the Seven Me's are constantly jostling for our attention. Depending on the situation, each Me can influence our behavior, actions, and decisions. Our challenge is to figure out which Me to allow to call the shots, to give the reins to, to allow to preside over the proceedings.

> Kind of like a rowdy group of kindergartners, the Seven Me's are constantly jostling for our attention.

Alignment of Our Senses of Self

In May 2003, behavioral expert Dr. Carol Adrienne, Ph.D., author of several books on self-discovery, discussed in an article what she calls the "syndrome of inauthenticity." According to Adrienne, the syndrome of inauthenticity occurs when our inner needs, values, and self-image don't match our outer expressions, behaviors, and accomplishments. In other words, this is what can happen when our Seven Me's are out of synch.

Sometimes, there can be a disconnect between the person we're trying to put out there for others (the Me I Try to Project) and the one we're trying to become (the Me I Want to Be). Or we struggle to incorporate or eliminate aspects of the person we've evolved from (the Me I Used to Be) with who we are now (the Me I Really Am or the Me I Think I Am). Perhaps, like my daughter's cheerleading coach, we're trying to grasp a more accurate view of our own self-perceptions (the Me I Think I Am) in terms of how others view us (the Me Others See). Maybe, we're challenged with how to accept input from others (the Me Others Try to Make Me) when that concept of self is different than our true selves (the Me I Really Am).

> There's not a human out there who has all their Seven Me's in exact alignment.

Whatever the case, there's not a human out there who has all their Seven Me's in exact alignment. And it's a rare individual who has them lined up with near-perfect consistency. In fact, this reflects an underlying goal of psychotherapy – to help people become congruent within themselves, to align their self-perceptions more accurately with the people they really are.

The closer our Seven Me's are to lining up with each other, the more at ease, in tune, and comfortable we are with ourselves. We take off the mask of the Me I Try to Project. There's not a black-and-white contrast between the Me I Used to Be, the Me I Think I Am, and the Me I Really Am. We're aware of the Me Others Try to Make Me and the Me Others See, and how filters are operating in ourselves and others. And we're constantly working on improving ourselves, so that the Me I Really Am lines up as much as possible with the Me I Want to Be.

Who's Calling the Shots?

Imagine you're the mother of a sixteen-year-old daughter, Lisa. She's your pride and joy – she makes good grades in school, is a star soccer player on the varsity team, and has a good group of friends whom you like. Aside from the requisite arguments here and there, the tumultuous teenage years haven't been all that difficult for you in raising your daughter. That is, until Lisa comes home from school one day, excitedly talking about Spring Break, which is just around the corner. Seems Lisa's three best friends are going to Panama City, Florida, for a week of sand, sun, and fun, and, *Oh please, Mom, can't I puh-leeeze, puh-leeze, PUH-LEEZE go, too?*

Hmm. This could be a tricky one. A bunch of teenagers in Panama City on their own for a week? With no parental supervision, hordes of hormone-infested adolescents, and parties galore, where alcohol (and maybe drugs) are likely to be present? On the other hand, Lisa has demonstrated that she's a trustworthy, dependable, responsible teenager. To the best of your knowledge, she's made good decisions to this point. And she would be going with her three best friends.

Oh, wait a second . . . Did I forget to mention that two of those best friends happen to be *seventeen-year-old guys?* Well, she might forget, too.

Let's take the bamboo tube away for just a second and look at the big picture of your Me's here. First of all, you have the **Me I Used to Be,** and, let's face it, that Me is one who spent a few crazy Spring Breaks of her own down in Panama City. You also have the **Me I Think I Am:** a parent who does a good job raising and disciplining her daughter, which falls closely in line with the **Me I Really Am:** a parent who *has* done a good job raising and disciplining her daughter, when measured by Lisa's successes and accomplishments in her sixteen years.

The **Me Others See,** in the eyes of Lisa, could be "*a way-cool Mom, one who's soooo awesome that she's letting me go to the beach with my buds! Whooo hooo!*", or one who's "*such an over-protective stick in the mud, who never, ever lets me do anything fun!*" And you have the **Me Others Try to Make Me,** again seen with respect to Lisa, whose needling and whining and persuading and begging are an attempt to shape you into one of those "super-cool, totally awesome" moms who let their children pretty much do whatever they want.

Let's not forget about the **Me I Try to Project,** which, depending on your decision, could be a parent with a firm stance on what is and isn't an acceptable situation for her daughter. Or it could be a parent who tries to be cool and laid back and really wants to be considered more of a friend than an authority figure.

Now, let's look at the **Me I Want to Be.** In line with this concept of self, what do you envision as your ideal behavior in this situation? You might want to be a parent who, well, really just wants to be *liked* by her daughter, so you tend to allow her more leverage and freedom than she's really ready for. Maybe you'd rather be a parent who takes the initiative to protect her daughter from herself, because at sixteen she just doesn't realize that going down to Panama City with her best girlfriend and two seventeen-year-old boys isn't an ideal scenario. I'm betting this also translates into a parent who, ultimately, will earn Lisa's respect when it counts because you were able to make decisions for her that she wasn't mature enough to make for herself.

For parents whose children haven't yet reached the tumultuous teenage years, these are the kind of decisions you might find yourself facing. (Though I wouldn't need much time to analyze my decision if my Lindsey, fifteen at the time this book went to press, should ever dare to approach me with such a request. Seven Me's, a quarter-second of thought, and one resounding *"NOT A SNOWBALL'S CHANCE IN THE BURNING DEPTHS OF HADES!"* would sum up everything quite nicely.)

But we don't usually dissect our interactions like this, analyzing which of our Me's are acting to influence us in different scenarios. Consequently, we often don't notice how each of our senses of self is operating all of the time, quietly percolating underneath the surface and helping to subtly shape our behavior. Our Seven Me's don't exist in a vacuum, operating independently of one another. Instead, they're constantly interacting, vying for space, jockeying for attention.

> Our Seven Me's don't exist in a vacuum, operating independently of one another. They're constantly interacting, vying for space, jockeying for attention.

The challenge, then, is to try to listen to each – and then figure out which one to give the reins to. More on that later, though. For now, let's take a look at what happens when our collective set of selves comes under fire, from ourselves and from those around us.

Chapter 12

The Infamous
Sidewalk Stumble

Blessed are those who can laugh at themselves,
for they shall never cease to be amused.
– Anonymous

*I*t's happened to each and every one of us: what I like to call
the Infamous Sidewalk Stumble. You're walking down the
street, minding your own business, heading to meet a friend
for lunch, off to an important business meeting, or just enjoy-
ing the weather on a lovely spring day, when *it* happens: You
trip and stumble, arms flailing as you somehow manage (thank
you, sweet Lord) to right yourself and regain your balance.

So what's the very first thing you do after you've inwardly
rejoiced about not actually busting butt on the pavement? If
you're like me and virtually any other human walking, er,
stumbling, the face of this earth, I'm betting you'll almost in-
stinctually glance around and see who else witnessed your
oh-so-ungraceful stride.

Why? Because your feathers are ruffled. Your ego is
bruised. You're embarrassed, flustered, and uncomfortable.
Your little stumble is a physical, unintentional act, but it
brings about a powerful emotional response in you, because
what you've just demonstrated does not represent a favorable
Me in your palette of selves. You have just harmed, bruised,
dented, and scratched your concepts of self.

Think about it: All seven of the Me's are affected. That's definitely not the Me I Try to Project. It's certainly not a favorable version of your Me Others See. Your Me I Used to Be? You learned to walk when you were one. It's likely not your Me I Think I Am. Your Me I Really Am can walk down the sidewalk. And it isn't even the Me Others Try to Make Me. Obviously, it's not the Me I Want to Be, either.

With that little trip on the pavement, all of your Seven Me's are somehow damaged a little bit. Your Infamous Sidewalk Stumble announced to the world: "I'm a klutzy, clumsy, uncoordinated doofus who doesn't have enough control over basic motor skills to make it down the sidewalk without tripping up." Unless you're one of those MTV tricksters like Johnny Knoxville that kids these days are so crazy about, you don't want to draw attention to yourself by stumbling, crashing, falling down, or maiming yourself in any of the ways Knoxville has become famous for. And you sure as heck don't want anyone else to be a witness to those actions, even if the others are strangers.

But if you're lucky enough that no one else has seen your little episode, it becomes a whole lot easier just to run your hands through your hair, smooth your shirt, and laugh the whole thing off, doesn't it? Our reasoning is that if no one else saw us stumble, we're okay. Our Seven Me's are still intact. *Trip on the sidewalk – who, me? Nobody saw anything. It didn't happen.*

We react as such because we're very protective of our Seven Me's. And when they are threatened – even by something as simple as our own clumsiness – we tend to lash out and redirect the blame or responsibility to other sources. Be honest: After you've looked around to see how many people saw you stumble, don't you immediately look down and look for the crack in the sidewalk? Or the little rock in your path? Or that spot where the pavement was uneven? You're searching for something, anything to be the explanation for why you tripped, because it simply *can't* be your own carelessness, can it?

Self-Defense Mechanisms

Psychologists call this phenomenon of lashing out, blaming, or redirecting a self-defense mechanism. We resort to this behavior many times when we are angry, embarrassed, or frustrated. Self-defense mechanisms are psychological ploys that the human mind resorts to in order to defend our Seven Me's by deceiving ourselves. Psychologists have identified as many as nineteen different behaviors classified as self-defense mechanisms, including compensation, stereotyping, displaced aggression, rationalization, apathy, repression, and fantasy – the list goes on and on. With a bag of tricks like this, we're incredibly quick to blame anyone or anything else for stupid things we've done in order to protect our Seven Me's.

> We're incredibly quick to blame anyone or anything else for stupid things we've done in order to protect our Seven Me's.

As a boy, I spent most of my afternoons playing in the backyard. We lived in a golf course community and our yard backed up to the green of hole number two – a tough hole. A number one handicap hole: long, narrow, and troublesome on both sides. This was a hole where handicaps went to die.

It was fun growing up on that hole. I learned a lot of colorful words listening to the golfers who played it. I witnessed the bruising of many a golfer's Seven Me's and the subsequent self-defense mechanisms they resorted to in order to try to defend and protect their concepts of self.

For example, I never knew putters could also serve as javelins. But after watching one guy miss an eighteen-inch putt for bogey on a hot summer afternoon, that's exactly what his putter was used as, flying fifty yards through the air in an impressive arc over the green.

> I never knew putters could also serve as javelins.

Missing that putt flew in the face of that golfer's Seven Me's. Like someone tripping on the sidewalk, or a baseball player missing the big pitch, he embarrassed himself and his concepts of self in front of others. His reaction? The self-defense mechanism of displaced aggression – it was the putter's fault, not his. And away it soared through the air.

The Spectrum of Slip-Ups

The missed putt and the infamous sidewalk stumble are just a few examples of millions of ways we can damage, destroy, and dent our Seven Me's. Some are more serious than others – the television program *America's Funniest Home Videos* is a hilarious showcase of those on the lighter side. On the more severe end, many psychologists and therapists are in business because their clients are experts in self-deprecation, self-degradation, and self-abuse.

Most of us slip up somewhere in the middle of that spectrum. We might mess up an important business presentation. Or turn into a stuttering, bumbling dolt on a first date. I could write another book documenting the ways I've goofed up just in my public speaking career. One time, I paced around the room unaware of my button-down shirt sticking a full three inches through my fly. Another time, during a break in a presentation, I went to the bathroom with my wireless microphone still on. Almost the entire audience I was speaking to heard those lovely tinkling sounds in stereo as they sipped their coffee and soda in the conference room where I had been speaking.

Perhaps the most memorable moment happened during a presentation several years ago. Early in my speech, I marched confidently toward the back of the stage, which was basically a large, raised platform. I was pointing to the impressive company banner stretched overhead, illustrating a point I can't even remember anymore. But as I walked, talked, and gestured (obviously, I should think twice about similar multi-tasking in the future), I failed to look down and notice the edge of the stage was right there. So I kept going and walked right off the stage, collapsing Coyote-style into a heap on the floor a few feet below. I wasn't hurt, thankfully, and it was also a miracle I didn't take down the banner, lighting, and sound system in one fell swoop. The real irony in my clumsiness: The group I was speaking to happened to be hundreds of safety executives.

> I went to the bathroom with my wireless microphone still on.

Suffice to say, my list of public stumbles is agonizingly long.

What's really interesting, though, is how in each of those instances my first reaction was to employ a self-defense mechanism for my own idiotic mistakes. When I traipsed around with my shirt through my fly, I whined to my wife about her letting me walk out of the house like that. When I went to the bathroom with my wireless mike still on, I wanted to blame the sound technician, but he'd shown me exactly how to operate the on/off switch long before the presentation started. When I walked off the stage, my first reaction was to wonder why nobody showed me around the platform, which had a layout plain as day for anyone to see – especially for someone who had given hundreds of presentations on similar stages throughout his career.

> To some degree, we all do this – damage our Seven Me's in one way or another and then look to pass the blame on to someone or something else.

To some degree, we all do this – damage our Seven Me's in one way or another and then look to pass the blame on to someone or something else. It's like the sales manager who chews out his sales team for slumping numbers because his boss, the VP, has just grilled him for a late report (that had nothing to do with the sales figures, by the way.) Or the harried parent who, in his hurry to pull the car into the garage on a rainy day, clips the garbage can on the way in – and then blames his kid for not leaving it in its usual spot six inches to the left.

Laugh and Live On

It's impossible to go through life without tripping up, without stumbling on the sidewalk every now and then. What's important, however, is not to try to avoid the cracks in the pavement, but to make sure we laugh at ourselves when we inevitably make a misstep. With some practice, we can learn not to take ourselves too seriously – which is an invaluable skill in living a fulfilling, happy life.

What is serious, though, is when our words or behaviors scratch, dent, or damage not our own Seven Me's, but those of others. When we do this – and sometimes we don't even realize that we're doing it – we're not establishing those satisfying, fulfilling koinonia connections we crave. Instead, we're building walls of separation that detract from our relationships, our experiences, and our quality of life.

> What is serious, though, is when our words or behaviors scratch, dent, or damage not our own Seven Me's but those of others.

Chapter 13

The Real Ouch

Expecting the world to treat you fairly because
you are a good person is a little like expecting the
bull not to attack you because you are a vegetarian.
– Dennis Wholey

As we learned in the previous chapter, it's one thing to say
or do stupid things that damage our own concepts of self. But,
when it comes to saying or doing things that harm, bruise,
dent, or scratch others' senses of self, it's an entirely different
dilemma. And it's where the real trouble starts in terms of
communicating with others.

Almost everyone is guilty of this – allowing negative, cutting, critical words to come out of our mouths, words that
scratch, bruise, and damage the Seven Me's of others. When
presenting to high school kids, I call these verbal attacks
"chops," insinuating that you've really "chopped" the legs out
from under someone, or you've "chopped" their ego. The
lingo also includes cuts, digs, or jabs. Whatever they're called,
they're ways we throw verbal sticks and stones.

These little things we say don't seem like that big of a deal,
but when they build up over time, every jab, each insult, and
every chop essentially kills a little piece of someone else's
soul, spirit, and self-worth. In fact, famous playwright Jules
Feiffer has wrapped an entire play around this concept of negativity. It's called "Little Murders."

From Pebbles to Boulders

These verbal sticks and stones can be small pebbles, carelessly tossed at someone in order to embarrass them: "Glad you could make it," the boss quips to one of her employees as he slinks into the team meeting ten minutes late. Or to demonstrate your quick wit: "Careful, your blonde roots are showing," a teenaged guy tells his girlfriend. Or to make yourself look or feel better: "Dude, you throw like a girl," a twelve-year-old boy tells his friend during gym in front of the entire class.

But sometimes, the sticks and stones can be logs and boulders that crush and kill the spirit of others. I'll never forget the time, at an annual meeting of a privately held company, I witnessed a vice president of customer service lambaste one particular manager in front of all the company's workers, upper-level executives, and shareholders because his was the only region that didn't hit its target numbers. I watched this man virtually shrivel up and die before my eyes as the vice president singled him out, circled in red marker on a poster how far he was below his target, and then threw the marker on the floor in disgust. "You'd better wake up and get your butt in gear," he warned before storming out, leaving the manager in stunned, embarrassed silence in front of the entire room.

> Sometimes, the sticks and stones can be logs and boulders that crush and kill the spirit of others.

Several years ago, my wife was selected as a candidate for jury duty. During the selection process, which can be a noto-

riously slow and boring affair, she became friendly with another woman, a nurse at a local hospital. With so much time
on their hands, my wife and this woman became fairly close
fairly quickly, chatting first about their personal interests and
children, and then sharing more serious stuff as the week pro-
gressed. By the end of their time together, this woman
confided to my wife one of the most debilitating examples of
sticks and stones I have ever heard.

The woman – who was quite attractive, my wife told
me – wanted to do something extra-special for her husband
for Father's Day. She picked out several gifts for him, but
ended up returning them because they didn't quite capture
the essence of what she wanted to express. She wanted
something a little more personal and meaningful, so she
decided to go to a professional photography studio and have
a portrait taken, wearing an elegant dress, makeup, hairdo,
the whole nine yards. She took the prints to work, where the
other nurses helped her pick out the best one. Then, she
bought a snazzy frame and matting for the chosen photo,
wrapped it beautifully, and hid it until Father's Day arrived.

But a few days before the holiday, she couldn't wait another second to present her husband with this gift she'd
poured her heart, soul, and energy into. So she gave it to him,
eagerly waiting his reaction as he pulled off the pretty paper.

He took one glance at his lovely wife in that photo and
said, "You look like a slut." He slammed the photo on the
kitchen counter and walked out of the room.

It was one of the biggest boulders I could imagine a husband saying to his wife, his life partner, and the mother of his
children. It's no wonder they eventually divorced.

Me, Myself, and I

I could go on for pages detailing examples of how words have damaged others and their Seven Me's, in varying degrees of extremes, drawing only upon my own personal experiences and those of people close to me. But it's a much more widespread problem than that. Our entire country is becoming addicted to this kind of negative communication. It's everywhere. In movies. On radio talk shows. On reality television. It's not just the media, either – you can step into high school cafeterias, corporate conference rooms, or family living rooms and witness the same kind of negativity. And the toll it is taking on our relationships is devastating.

> Our entire country is becoming addicted to this kind of negative communication. It's everywhere.

So why do we do it?

Psychologists say we spend about 93-96 percent of our time worrying about ME: *my* job, *my* bank account, *my* upcoming promotion, *my* car, *my* project that's due next week, *my* progress in yoga class, *my* next meal, what am I going to say, how am *I* going to look, *me, me, me, I, I, I, mine, mine, mine.* Trevor Turner, a writer with *New Internationalist,* nailed it when he wrote in the April 2003 issue: "Today, a rising tide of narcissism is spreading like a toxic social algae." For those of you like me who slept through Latin class, the word "narcissism" comes from the Greek myth of a stunningly handsome boy, Narcissus, who spent all of his time admiring his reflection in a pond. Eventually, he fell in and drowned. (Narcissus was Greek, all right, but I'd bet his life was painfully lacking in koinonia connections.)

If, in fact, we spend 93-96 percent of our time worrying about Me like modern-day narcissists, that leaves less than ten percent of our remaining time to think about other people, about their emotional, psychological, and behavioral needs. Those other people aren't just the nameless, faceless masses out there. They're the individuals we work with, we live with, and we interact with on a daily basis. They're our colleagues. Our spouses. Our children. Our friends. They are the people we want and need koinonia connections with.

But aren't our own lives – those with which we're so obsessed – directly influenced and affected by our relationships with those other people? So, from a purely ego-centric standpoint, wouldn't it make sense to put a little more thought and effort into the well-being of others? That is, to really take a hard look into how our actions and words affect them – which could in turn change our own lives for the better?

Sad to say, all too often this logic escapes us. We're so adept at and attuned to thinking about our own needs that we inadvertently toss sticks and stones without even realizing it, tearing down others' Seven Me's with no idea about the consequences of our actions. We chastise our child for his C+ on the math test (without acknowledging his progress from the previous D-). We point out that our employee missed her sales target for this month (without remembering she hit or exceeded the mark for the last six months). We snap at the grocery store clerk for not double-bagging our purchases (without realizing it's his second day on the job). We're so quick to wield our sticks and toss our stones without realizing we're missing a chance to drop our weapons and offer a helpful word of encouragement instead.

> We're so adept at and attuned to thinking about our own needs that we inadvertently toss sticks and stones without even realizing it.

Human Nature?

We're not entirely to blame, though, at least not for the bio-physical processes that can lead us to lose control of what comes out of our mouths. As humans, we have a biochemical reaction that kicks in when we're angry or upset. Our bodies are equipped with an automatic defense system called the "fight or flight mechanism." This efficient system preps us for action – whether we're going to fight and resist the instigating force facing us, or flee by escaping from the situation.

When our emotions are kicked into high gear with anger, fear, or hostility, more adrenaline is pumped into our bloodstream. This, in turn, sets off a series of physiological responses within our bodies, transforming a calm parent into a red-faced father, snorting fire from his nostrils, streaming smoke from his ears. With Dad-turned-demon in this state, I wouldn't want to be anywhere near earshot of the sticks, stones, boulders, and rocks that are likely to tumble out of his mouth.

> However, even in these heightened emotional states, we still have ultimate responsibility over what we say.

However, even in these heightened emotional states, we still have ultimate responsibility over what we say. Many of us have heard the strategy of stopping and counting to ten (or to 10,000, if you have to!). Distancing ourselves from the situation is another idea. Over the years, my wife and I have developed our own special way of calming down when tensions rise. If an argument is becoming too heated, we'll sit down, look each other in the eyes, and hold hands while trying to make our respective points. For us, holding hands is a very powerful reminder that our love and commitment to each other are more important than whatever issue we're arguing about. Granted, we don't do this every time we fight. But when we make the effort, this little trick almost always works – and we rarely walk away still angry or regretting something we've said to each other.

Coping strategies are good for what they're worth, but ultimately we have to realize we must take control of the most powerful muscle in our bodies – our tongue. It weighs so little, but so few of us can hold it.

The following poem illustrates the incredible power of the tongue.

The Tongue

The boneless Tongue, so small and weak,
Can crush and kill, declared the Greek.
The Tongue destroys a greater horde,
The Turk asserts, than does the sword.
A Persian proverb wisely saith,
A lengthy Tongue, an early death.
Or sometimes takes this form instead,
Don't let your Tongue cut off your head.
The Tongue can speak a word whose speed,
Say the Chinese, outstrips the steed.
While Arab sages this impart:
The Tongue's great storehouse is the heart.
From Hebrew wit the maxim sprung,
Though the feet should slip, ne'er let the Tongue.
The sacred writer crowns the whole:
Who keeps the Tongue doth keep the soul.

– Anonymous

Tips for Taming Your Tongue

With some practice, we can learn to control what comes out of our mouths. The following are four simple questions we can ask ourselves before we open them – and before we have a chance to throw any sticks or stones.

1) Is what you're about to say kind? This one is so simple, but so effective. Will it tear down, scratch, harm, or dent someone else and their Seven Me's? If so, don't share it.

2) Is it true? The more layers the information is passed through, the less likely it is to be completely accurate. If you heard it from someone, who heard it from someone else, who heard it from someone's neighbor's boss's sister-in-law's friend, it's likely lost some of its truthfulness and gained quite a bit of embellishment. If you can't check the source, don't share it.

3) Is it confidential? If you have to start a sentence by saying, "I shouldn't be telling you this, but . . ." *DON'T!* You're completely betraying the trust of whoever confided in you. And that's the fastest way you can move away from those ideal koinonia connections we need and crave in our lives.

4) Is it necessary? Where is it written that the abundance of words is a good thing? Does the other person need to know what you're about to share? Or is your Me I Try to Project – a person who's in-the-know and part of the loop and always up-to-date about what's going on – taking over again?

Silent Sticks and Stones

As important as it is to control our tongues, there are times when the most damaging sticks and stones we throw don't come out of our mouths. In fact, they don't make a sound at all. But they can have consequences devastating enough to render us speechless.

Take a look at the heartbreaking story of Justin, a twelve-year-old in South Florida. Justin was so afraid about being teased for his weight problem on the first day of school that he couldn't bear the thought of going to class. So he took a rope into his family's backyard. As the household bustled to get ready for the day, Justin was nowhere to be found – until his two little brothers went looking for him in the backyard and found him dangling from the branches, the rope around his broken neck. Justin's father cut his lifeless body from the tree and tried to revive his son, but it was too late. "Sticks and stones may break your bones, but names will never hurt you," as the maxim goes? Well, in Justin's case, just the *prospect* of the sticks and stones he feared would come flying at him at school that day – combined with those that had probably been piled on him throughout his twelve years – essentially stripped the life out of his young body.

> There are times when the most damaging sticks and stones we throw don't come out of our mouths.

Several years ago in Japan, little Keiji took the plate during his team's season-ending playoff game. It was the bottom of the final inning, with two outs, two on base, and his team behind by one run. Keiji gritted his teeth, gripped the bat, and ambled to the plate. The pitcher wasted no time in blistering the first strike. The blood rushed through Keiji's head like a freight train. Sweat dripped from his furrowed brow. He scuffed his shoes in the dirt and stepped back to the plate, the pitcher's eyes boring through him like lasers before he wound up again. Strike two.

Keiji swallowed hard. This was it. He'd get a hit, make it to first; even a walk would be great. *Anything* but striking out. Keiji felt the weight of hundreds of expectant eyes, in the stands and on the field, all focused on him. Oh, this wasn't just a game, all right. This was pure agony.

There came the pitch, sweet, low, and right over the plate, just where Keiji liked it . . . He put every ounce of his being into his bat, pulling it around and praying for the glorious sensation of contact . . . *THOCK.* The ball cracked into the catcher's mitt with a deadly thud.

Strike three. Game over.

The opposing team erupted, players bursting out of the dugout like freshly popped champagne, showering the pitcher with hugs and high-fives. At the same time, you could almost see Keiji's team deflate, players dropping their heads, their eyes, and their mitts with the weight of defeat.

Keiji's heart sank to his shoes. He turned his eyes, welling with hot tears, to his teammates, desperately seeking solace in their faces – a sympathetic glance, a look saying "It's okay," a smile of support. He got nothing except glares.

Close to panic now, silently begging for any ounce of comfort, any hint of reassurance, any shred of acknowledgement, Keiji looked to his coach, the one who'd taught him to swing, how to steal second, how to handle a hard grounder. Surely his coach would come to his rescue.

His coach looked away, turning his back in dead silence.

Keiji then turned on his heel and fled from this storm of silent sticks and stones. Once home, he went into the garage and hanged himself, like Justin on the other side of the globe.

Removing the Bamboo Tube

I realize the above examples are extremes, and with each story there are other factors to consider than just the silent sticks and stones that were cast – cultural differences in the story of Keiji, for example, and possible depression issues with Justin. Still, both scenarios paint a very grim picture about the extreme gravity and consequences our words and actions can have on the lives of others.

It's also easy to consider the position of the baseball coach and distance ourselves from his situation – reading that story, we might say, *I would never behave that way if I was a coach.* But let's once again remove the bamboo tube for just a minute, and look at our lives from a broader perspective.

While the coach literally turned his back on Keiji, have we ever done the same thing in a figurative sense? Have we looked the other direction when a simple gesture of kindness would have changed the outcome drastically? Have we kept our mouths shut instead of offering a word of encouragement, or even just a smile? These are things we've all been guilty of at one point or another. But like that coach, I doubt we would repeat our behavior if we were able to take away the bamboo tube and consider the big-picture impact of our words and actions on the situation.

Chapter 14

Sticks, Stones, and Kissing Frogs

Kind words can be short and easy to speak,
but their echoes are truly endless.
- Mother Teresa

*I*t's a scientific fact, as well as a fun trivia tidbit to throw out at parties, that if you drop a frog into a pot of boiling water, he'll jump right back out. He wants no part of that environment. But if you put the same frog into a pot of room temperature water and slowly keep turning up the heat, it's gonna be frog legs for dinner. That poor little amphibian will keep adjusting and adapting to the increasing heat without knowing it will eventually kill him.

People struggle with the same challenge – the inability to discern small, incremental changes in their emotional and relationship environments. And just like that frog slowly dies, so too do the hearts and spirits of people every day when those changes are negative.

We're just like frogs. If you drop us into a situation that's hot and fiery from the start – a prickly work group, a rude receptionist, or a mean classmate on the playground – we back off immediately. Like the frog, we instantly recognize the harmful environment, and we want no part of it.

But it's the slow simmer that kills us, too.

Have you ever been assigned to a project team, and when you showed up for the first meeting, the temperature of the room felt okay? The other team members all seemed like fine people to work with. You didn't know them very well, but there didn't appear to be any stone throwers in the group.

But one day, months into the project, you show up at the weekly team meeting and it hits you – *I can't stand being here.*

What happened? you wonder. *How did all of a sudden I get to this state?* The thing is, you didn't just get here. This situation had been simmering all along, but you hadn't noticed.

> People's hearts, souls, and spirits are slowly perishing, and they don't even realize it until they're completely cooked.

What began as a "normal" project team environment twisted into a negative, needling, nitpicky group, one that was sucking the life out of you every day. But when you try to put your finger on exactly when this shift took place, it's impossible to pinpoint one person, issue, or incident that caused it. All you know is, like that frog, you're completely fried.

The same thing happens every day in families, companies, schools, fraternities . . . The list goes on and on. People's hearts, souls, and spirits are slowly perishing, and they don't even realize it until they're completely cooked.

Sticks, Stones, and Straw

Surely you've heard the expression "the straw that broke the camel's back." What we're talking about is pretty much the same thing – but instead of straw, it's sticks and stones. Years and years of puny pebbles and tiny twigs have taken a big toll on many marriages, friendships, and working relationships.

And when this happens, whether we're the one doing the tossing or the one who's the target, we – and our relationships – are both in hot water, just like the frog in the pot.

But, just as it took a lot of straw to break that camel's back, it takes a lot of sticks and stones to reach this boiling point. Marriages don't explode into divorce; they erode into discontent and disconnection as partners move farther and farther from the koinonia ideal. The communication gap between parents and children doesn't split instantaneously like an earthquake that reads a ten on the Richter scale. It starts as a small crack that eventually widens into a seemingly impassible gorge. Co-workers who don't get along rarely have a knock-down, drag-out rumble in the break room. Instead, their hostility simmers and bubbles through a slow boil of disapproving looks across the office, rolled eyes during meetings, and avoidance in the halls.

Years and years of puny pebbles and tiny twigs have taken a big toll on many marriages, friendships, and working relationships.

Frogs and Fairy Tales

To this point, we've spent lots of time discussing the truth behind a well-intentioned but misguided childhood rhyme: Sticks and stones may break your bones, but names will never hurt you. We've discovered just how untrue and counterproductive that rhyme really is, and the ways in which our words really *do* hurt.

In these last sections, we're going to take one more trip back to our childhood days, when make-believe and pretending were a big part of our lives. We heard stories about frogs back then, too. Don't we all remember the fairy tale of the frog, the princess, and the witch? You know the story: A handsome prince runs into a mean, nasty witch, who pulls out her wand and casts a spell, turning him – *ZAP!* – into a sad, lonely frog. The only thing that can break the spell is a kiss from a princess. And, as fate would have it, a princess happens to be walking through the forest that day. She picks up the frog, kisses him – *SMACK!* – right on his lips, and – *POOF!* – he turns back into a prince, and they live happily ever after.

Here's where the old fairy tale takes a modern-day twist. It's not really a fairy tale – it's a metaphor for life, and how we interact with one another. And believe it or not, we've all, at one point or another, played all three roles in the story.

How many times have we been the frog – feeling sad, lonely, and hopeless? Instead of a spell cast upon us, sticks and stones did the damage. Just as the witch's spell made the prince feel sad, lonely, and hopeless, verbal sticks and stones do the same thing to us.

The world today is full of frogs.

What about the witch? Just as she cast a spell that negatively influenced the life of another, so too have we – not with wands, but with words. Our verbal sticks and stones can be just as evil as a spell, harming and hurting the life of another.

And then, there's the princess – who could have easily strolled right past the frog, but instead, stopped, picked him up, and made the conscious decision to make his day a little brighter. The impact of her miniscule gesture was a life-changing event for the frog as the spell was broken and he changed back into a prince.

The world today is full of frogs. They can be easy to recognize, like Damien, the third-grader we talked about, or Keiji, the Little Leaguer who struck out. Sometimes, like Justin, they're more difficult to spot. But it's important to realize that we and everyone around us – our spouses, children, co-workers, friends, customers, clients, the guy selling newspapers at the traffic light – can be frogs, negatively affected by the unkind words of others.

In the same way we don't recognize the prince when he's in frog form, we often don't recognize when others around us have been zapped. With the same energy it takes to step over them (or, even worse, *on* them) and continue on our way, wouldn't it be just as easy to drop our sticks, put down our stones, and pick those frogs up with some encouraging, uplifting, supportive affirmations?

What the world needs today is more frog kissers. Like that princess, frog kissers don't stroll past or step over the frogs in their paths. Instead, they intentionally choose, through their words and actions, to support, encourage, and affirm those with whom they come in contact.

Do you remember the first Rocky movie? Rocky was a frog kisser. You can tell by watching Adrienne.

When Adrienne's character was introduced into the movie, she was a frog in every sense of the word. Of course, I don't mean she had slimy green skin and long, spindly legs. But every aspect of her appearance – from her hunched, cowering posture, to her thick knit cap, to her dark clothes and black-rimmed glasses – sent the message that Adrienne didn't value

What the world needs today is more frog kissers.

herself as a person. She had obviously run into a witch or two somewhere in her life.

Enter Rocky. From the day he stepped into the pet store where she worked, Rocky began to be a positive influence on Adrienne. He loved her just as she was. He accepted her just as she was. And as a result of Rocky's accepting Adrienne, Adrienne began accepting Adrienne.

For perhaps the first time in her life, Adrienne ran into a frog kisser. And her transformation was crystal clear in the final scene of the movie, when she burst into the boxing arena, a strong, confident, beautiful woman, those glasses and knit cap gone, a stylish beret perched on her head, as she plowed through the maddening crowds to embrace her man. Adrienne was a princess in the eyes of anybody watching.

Frog Kissing 101

We all know Rocky wasn't the brightest bulb in the chandelier, but he was nevertheless a frog kisser. Anybody can be one. It doesn't require a college degree, lots of life experience, or hours of meditation. It begins with the simple step of what I call "looking for ways to praise." This concept lies at the heart of frog kissing.

Do we look for ways to praise?

We have a choice with every interaction we make. Do we look for ways to praise by choosing words that uplift, encourage, and affirm? Or do we pick up sticks and stones, criticizing, condemning, and cutting down? Let me give you an example of how simple – yet powerful – this choice can be.

Let's sneak a peak into a typical family household during breakfast. In my home growing up, the kitchen was always a whirlwind of activity in the morning. In fact, we even called my mom the Great White Tornado. She tore through the kitchen in her white bathrobe, simultaneously making breakfast for the five of us and lunch for my dad and us three kids – nine meals in all. At the same time, she was checking that socks matched, teeth were brushed, and no belt loops were missed, all while keeping an eye on the clock to ensure Dad made it to the office and we made it to the bus stop on time.

Amidst this frenzy one morning, my dad decided he wanted another cup of coffee.

"Hey, Fats, how about another cup of coffee, on the double?" he barked at my mom, who snapped around from the sink sharply enough to give herself whiplash.

"*What* did you say?" Mom snarled back at him. In that moment, my dad's rude, careless, cutting demand turned her into a frog, and she was one angry amphibian, all right.

He fired something right back at her, and a squabble ensued that sent us kids off and running for the school bus just to get away from the flurry of sticks and stones in the kitchen. I remember running just as fast *to* the bus stop as I did running home *from* it that cold winter day I was called Shrimpus by my classmates.

Fast forward to the same scenario a few weeks later. The Great White Tornado, again ripping a swatch through the kitchen, my dad gulping his last sip of coffee. Again, he opens his mouth: "Hey, F—."

My dad paused.

At that instant, I watched him have a *déjà vu* moment. His entire countenance changed. In that second, instead of carelessly cutting my mother down, he made a conscious decision to affirm both her and her coffee. Like the sun coming out from behind the clouds, a smile spread across my father's face, his brow unfurrowed, and he exclaimed, "Hey Miss America, how about some more of that great coffee?"

You should have seen my mom.

She coyly turned from the sink, the grin on her face bright enough to melt the snow outside. "You devil, you!" she cooed, her eyes sparkling. She sidled up to my father, poured him another cup of joe, and poured herself right into his lap. The next thing I knew, that kitchen was full of hugs, kisses, and koinonia all over the place. For an eight-year-old, it was disgusting. And just like the last time, my brother, sister, and I were outta there, off and running for the bus stop.

Frog Kissing and King Solomon

Do you see the difference in those two scenarios? Do you see how such a simple shift in behavior can bring about such completely different outcomes?

I had not thought about those two scenes in my kitchen for more than twenty-five years. Until, one quiet morning while reading, I came across a familiar quote whose significance I hadn't been able to grasp until that exact moment. In the words of King Solomon (Proverbs 18:21): "The tongue has the power of life and death, and those who love it will eat its fruit." I had read that saying dozens of times and never really understood what it meant. But for some reason that particular morning, I was transported back to my family's kitchen nearly twenty-five years earlier. And I finally understood what Solomon knew all along.

Let's dissect those two scenarios in my kitchen.

"Hey Fats, how about another cup of coffee on the double?" Obviously, those were words of death. What was the fruit – the outcome? Anger. Resentment. Bitterness. Fighting, enough so that we three kids fled the room to avoid being collateral damage, lest we get pegged by a stray stick or stone.

Three weeks later: *"Hey Miss America, how about some more of that great coffee?"* Obviously, these were words of life – uplifting, affirming, encouraging. The fruit? Hugging. Kissing. Laughing. Sharing. Koinonia. We kids still fled the room, but for a completely different reason this time (wink, wink).

Without knowing it, my father experienced the truth in Solomon's insight about the incredible power of our words and their profound impact on our relationships. In those two mornings in my family's kitchen, my dad went from a stone thrower to a frog kisser.

Frog Kissing and the Key Me

My father may not have realized it at the time, but when he called my mother "Miss America" and asked her for some more "great" coffee, he stumbled upon the key component of frog kissing. You see, while you can begin to develop the skill of frog kissing by doing something as simple as complimenting another person or looking for something kind to say, true frog kissing goes a little deeper. It involves the dynamics of the Seven Me's that we discussed earlier. You remember them:

- ○ The Me I Think I Am
- ○ The Me I Really Am
- ○ The Me I Used to Be
- ○ The Me Others See

- ◯ The Me I Try to Project
- ◯ The Me Others Try to Make Me
- ◯ The Me I Want to Be

We learned how there's a power struggle going on with those Seven Me's. They all want to influence the situation. As demonstrated in the dilemma with Lisa, the teenager who wanted to go to Panama City for Spring Break, the Seven Me's are always jockeying for position, both in ourselves and in those with whom we interact.

Our challenge, then, is twofold. First, we need to figure out which of those Seven Me's within ourselves to give the reins to. The one to put in the driver's seat. The one who will take control of our words and our behaviors. Second, we have to do the same with others – determine which of those Seven Me's to bring out, communicate with, or inspire.

> The Key Me is the Me I Want to Be.

This might sound like a daunting task, with all those Me's running around. But it's actually quite simple. What my dad accidentally stumbled onto, and what we need to grasp, is that the Key Me is the Me I Want to Be. It's the one we need to give control to in our own palette of Me's, and the one we need to connect with in others.

If I had asked my father twenty-five years ago what kind of a husband he wanted to be, it's safe to say he would have expressed something along the lines of a loving husband, a caring husband, a husband who appreciates, affirms, and compliments his wife. But his behavior did not always reflect that ideal, especially when he said things like "Hey Fats, how about another cup of coffee, on the double?"

Which Me was in control at that moment? Perhaps the Me I Used to Be, a former West Point coach accustomed to ordering cadets around. Maybe it was the Me I Try to Project, a powerful CEO always used to getting his way. Whichever Me might have been influencing his behavior, it was definitely not the Me I Want to Be as a husband.

Let's again jump ahead three weeks, to virtually the exact same scenario. The same time, the same scene, the same people, even the same request: more coffee. But a completely different Me was in control of the situation – the Me I Want to Be, the one which encompassed my father's highest goals and ideals for himself as a husband, one who appreciated his wife's efforts and appearance: "Hey Miss America, how about some more of that great coffee?" With this simple comment, my dad handed the reins to the Me I Want to Be.

Just as the Me I Want to Be was the Key Me for my father in that second scenario, it was also the Key Me for him to connect with in my mom. If I'd asked her what was her Me I Want to Be as the CEO of our household, again it's safe to say she'd share something along the lines of a loving mother and wife who demonstrated that love through hearty breakfasts, handmade lunches, and hugs in the morning. And that's exactly the Me my father was speaking to the second time around. Judging by the reaction he got from my mom, it's pretty obvious how he chose to ask for his second cup of coffee from that morning on.

The Fine Art of Frog Kissing

This is the underlying challenge of frog kissing – allowing the Me I Want to Be to take the lead in our own Seven Me's, while communicating to the Me I Want to Be in others. It happened in my kitchen that day, and it can happen everywhere, every day, in everyone's life.

Lonnie Edwards, a teacher at an elementary school outside of Atlanta, was a frog kisser.

One day during gym class, Mr. Edwards, a physical education teacher, was showing his students the basics of square dancing. He chose little Nancy as his partner to help demonstrate some of the steps, but she refused, backing away and starting to cry. Mr. Edwards pulled Nancy away from the other students to see if he could figure out what the problem was and only then realized what she'd amazingly been able to hide: a pair of hands that were unusually formed, with only a thumb and pinky on each. Still, while Nancy managed to conceal her hands from teachers by keeping them under a small towel she carried and by making good grades in class, the other students knew, and ridiculed and harassed her relentlessly.

Mr. Edwards was shocked when he saw Nancy's hands for the first time in gym class that day. But he slowly took the towel from the girl, put it in his back pocket, and never gave it back. Instead, he took her hands, danced with her in gym class that day, and eventually, the other students wanted to dance with her too.

Nancy, now a wife and mother of four children, learned to play the piano and type at sixty words a minute. She and Mr. Edwards were eventually re-united on a tearful talk show, where she told the audience how much her teacher's support and encouragement meant to her.

Mr. Edwards' Key Me, the Me I Want to Be, was the kind of teacher who truly wanted to make a positive impact on a child. One who supported, encouraged, and helped his students achieve their highest potential. For Nancy, the Key Me was a third-grader just like all the other boys and girls in her class. One who didn't have to hide her hands. One who could square dance with the other kids in gym class. That was exactly the Me that Mr. Edwards spoke to when he took away Nancy's towel and took her hands to dance with her that day. And as Nancy told the television audience decades later, his words and behavior had a profound effect on her life.

What's in it For Me?

About halfway through writing this book, I had an appointment with the doctor on a Friday morning. I wasn't exactly thrilled about starting my day with needles and tests, but I put on a bright face nonetheless and headed into the doctor's office, where I waited at the receptionist's desk for one, two, nearly three full minutes (I glanced discreetly at my watch) while the receptionist sat clacking away at her computer, not even addressing me.

I'll admit after the first minute or so, I wanted to reach over and tap the little bell on the counter a few times to let her know I was there – and not happy about being kept waiting – but I managed to restrain myself. Finally, without an "I'll be with you in just a moment" or a nod or even a grunt of acknowledgement, the receptionist finally looked up, asked my name, and checked me in. Despite my irritation, I remained polite, smiling and saying, "Thank you very much," after she entered my info into the computer. I sat down in the waiting room and leafed through a magazine until I was called in a few minutes later.

After my appointment with the doctor, I went back to the receptionist to take care of my bill. When I walked up, she was leaving a message for a patient about completing a satisfaction survey. Her voice was pleasant, cheerful – and completely the opposite of her hostile demeanor a while earlier.

But I didn't point out that Jekyll-and-Hyde turnaround. Instead, I remarked, "You know, that was a nice, efficient message you just left. If I was the person receiving it, I would definitely return that call, even if it is for something like a survey."

The receptionist's eyes lit up. A huge grin broke out across her face, and she couldn't hide the look of surprise that had taken over her. "Well, thank you so much," she replied, her smile still glowing as she printed up my bill. My words – just two quick sentences of praise – flipped a switch in her attitude. I was speaking to her competence as an employee, which coincided with her Me I Want to Be as the most efficient, courteous receptionist she could be, and that's exactly how she treated me for the remainder of my time, although brief, in the office. Furthermore, I'll bet the next time I have an appointment, she wouldn't dream of letting me stand in front of her desk for even ten seconds before checking me in.

My words flipped a switch in her attitude.

Therein lies another aspect of frog-kissing: the end result, which is often a bonus for the frog kisser. Just as the princess was rewarded with a handsome prince after she kissed the frog, frog-kissing often elicits a response in the other person that's also beneficial to us. My father was treated to a shower of kisses and loving attention from my mother after his frog-kissing comments in asking for more coffee. The receptionist was infinitely nicer to me after my kind, frog-kissing words. In two very different scenarios, my father and I both gained immediate positive benefits from our decision to frog-kiss.

When we frog kiss we're building bridges of connectedness and stronger koinonia connections.

However, the big-picture reward is much more significant. Frog kissing is a critical element in moving forward on the koinonia continuum with others. When we throw sticks and stones, we're tearing down our relationships. When we frog kiss, we do the opposite: We're building bridges of connectedness and stronger koinonia connections. And as we all know by now, those koinonia connections form the basis of satisfying relationships and happier lives.

Everyday Frog Kissing

While I was doing research for this book, a friend passed along a column I found incredibly relevant to the topics I was looking into. The writer, Julie Nichols, is a former columnist for the *Northwest Florida Daily News* and a college English professor.

"Shadows Can Touch Other Souls"

Our tai chi group held practice outdoors last week in a small clearing in the woods. As we stood in the silence of the trees and the breeze, the shadow of a small airplane swept over us.

How interesting, I thought, that the plane's shadow just happened to touch our group. Someone else mentioned it later, and we'd all noticed.

The pilot was no doubt unaware of our brief connection, just as we're all often unaware of how easily we touch each other.

Later, when I stopped for a quick lunch, the speaker at the burger drive-through was on the fritz, and the kid on the other end sounded like a whale in a punk-rock band. I couldn't understand anything he was saying. When I paid him, he was sullen and smirky, and I got snappish about the speaker. I drove off irritated, and left him the same way, I'm sure. What was his mood when he served the next customer? A little humor and kindness on both our parts would have changed the direction of both our days.

Sometimes, the impact of a seemingly minor gesture lasts a lot longer. About 15 years ago, University of West Florida instructor Mamie Hixon wrote on my paper, "You're really bringing your average up." I'd been struggling in the course, and I felt so pleased when I read her words. That simple comment on my paper has been passed on countless times on my own students' papers.

Some years ago, one of my students wrote about her bout with anorexia. She said it all started when she was eating macaroni and cheese and her boyfriend introduced her to someone as "chubby." The macaroni turned to paste in her mouth. From then on, she couldn't eat without thinking of being fat. It took years of therapy for her to regain her health.

I wonder how many people have dismissed their own worth or dreams because of a single comment from someone important to them.

"Don't you think you should lay off the French fries?"

"That's a stupid idea."

We're really very fragile creatures, we humans, so needful of acceptance and love, so impressionable and so careless with each other.

I still recall the incident that soured me on big cities. I was 19 years old, on my own and visiting Chicago. I was trying to get on the train and didn't understand the token system or the turnstile. An impatient worker said, "Look, lady, you just put the token in the slot here."

She had dismissed me as a nameless moron. Her words and tone lingered and blended with the jumble of noise and people who looked right through me. When I finally got off the train in Rantoul, a small town with more cornstalks than people, I was much relieved.

Every encounter we have with another person changes that person's life, maybe for a moment, maybe forever. And it happens as briefly and easily as a shadow passing over us.

Frog Kissing Forever

As Nichols so eloquently put it, we have a choice in every encounter with another person. Whether it's at the breakfast table with our family, at the conference table with our co-workers, or, like Nichols, at the burger drive-through with a smirky teenager, we can choose to throw sticks and stones, or we can choose to frog-kiss. It all boils down to a choice we make in every interaction we have with someone else.

Frog kissing is addictive and contageous.

Frog kissing is addictive and contagious. Once you begin to see its power for yourself, you'll want to try it everywhere: in the office, at home, in the gym, even on the street. And after you do, you'll notice a positive difference in your relationships – and ultimately, in your life. You'll begin to experience the true meaning of koinonia.

Along the way, be aware that you'll occasionally meet a person who doesn't respond to your frog-kissing efforts. You know the type. They're constantly bitter. They're perpetual stone-throwers. They look like their faces have been baptized in prune juice. No amount of uplifting, affirming, encouraging words and behaviors on your part seems to make a difference with these kind of people. But don't let your occasional encounters with these types sour you on the potential of frog-kissing. If you do, you'll rob yourself and others around you of its life-changing impact.

I guarantee you'll come across at least one frog a day. And when you do, will you be a stone-thrower, or a frog-kisser?

The choice is yours. Choose wisely. It's a wonderful trip to make progress on purpose.

End Notes

"Hurtful Words Can Have Physical Effect, Says UConn Researcher," by Karen Grava. Office of University Communications, University of Connecticut, Storrs. August 16, 1999. http://www.news.uconn.edu/1999/aug1999/rel99010.htm

"If I Could Turn Back Time," by Cher, written by Diane Warren. *Cher's Greatest Hits,* Geffen Records. Originally released in 1988.

Scripture taken from the New King James Version. Copyright 1982 by Thomas Nelson, Inc. Used by permission. All rights reserved.

"Aggravating Circumstances: A Status Report on Rudeness in America." Conducted by Public Agenda, a nonprofit research arm of The Pew Charitable Trusts. http://www.pewtrusts.com/pdf/vf_public_agenda_rude.pdf

A 2001 poll commissioned by www.wordscanheal.org. http://www.wordscanheal.org/press/pressRelease_poll.htm

Men Are From Mars, Women Are From Venus: A Practical Guide for Improving Communication and Getting What You Want in Your Relationships, by John Gray. HarperCollins, 1992.

I'm OK, You're OK: A Practical Guide to Transactional Analysis, by Thomas Harris. Avon Books, 1973.

"Singles." Written and directed by Cameron Crowe. Warner Bros., 1992.

http://www.forgiving.org, website for A Campaign for Forgiveness Research.

Alice's Adventures in Wonderland, by Lewis Carroll. First published by MacMillan, London, in 1865.

"Authenticity," by Carol Adrienne. www.soulfulliving. com/authenticity.html. May 2003.

"I Shop, Therefore I Am–Privatization: Narcissm," by Trevor Turner. *New Internationalist.* April 2003.

"Boy fears teasing on his weight, kills self," by Deborah Sharp. *USA Today.* Aug. 27, 1996. pg. A4.

"The Power of Kindness," by Doug Cumming. *The Atlanta Journal-Constitution.* Oct. 9, 1996. pg. C1.

HOLY BIBLE, NEW INTERNATIONAL VERSION.
Copyright 1973, 1978. The International Bible Society,
used by permission of Zondervan Bible Publishers.

"Shadows Can Touch Other Souls," by Julie Nichols.
Northwest Florida Daily News. March 28, 2004, pg. E1.

STICKS & STONES ... and more!

Author Dave Weber is president of Weber Associates, a training and consulting company based in Atlanta, Georgia. An internationally recognized speaker, Weber conducts training and motivational programs for thousands of people every year in organizations such as:

- The Weather Channel
- FedEx
- Chick-fil-A
- Cintas
- Bank of America
- Delta Airlines
- and many others

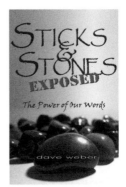

To contact Dave Weber or Weber Associates regarding additional copies of *Sticks and Stones Exposed: The Power of Our Words* visit: **www.sticksandstonesexposed.com**.

If you are interested in speaking engagements, or to request additional information about Weber Associates, please visit: **www.weberassociates.com**.

You can also call **1-800-800-8184** or **770-422-5654**.

WEBER ASSOCIATES
make progress on purpose

975 Cobb Place Blvd.
Suite 107
Kennesaw, GA 30144
1-800-800-8184
www.weberassociates.com